⚙⚙⚙

"Alaina is a true creative spirit. Her poignant story is told with candor and humor and is illustrative of the social miseries proliferated whenever the grip of patriarchal theology squeezed. Even today conventional religious up-bringing can injure a woman's sense of self worth, but her example of living fully in the present now, shows how it is possible to bounce back. Her pioneer spirit as described in the book is alive and well."

"[Alaina,] keep on writing and dancing your way through life. I look forward to your next book."

—**Shirae Rogers Curd**, RN (Ret.) *a friend and advocate.*

⚙⚙⚙

". . . your descriptions were so realistic I felt I was right there experiencing it."

— **Louise Thomas,** Hurricane, UT

⚙⚙⚙

"Thank goodness there are people who remain faithful to the craft of preserving the past, so that those who follow will be able to touch the foot prints and feel the heartbeats of those who went this way before us. In Black Rocks and Cold Wind, Alaina Newhart has done this with grace and style."

***—Al Cooper**, Author:* **Fortifying Your Home Against The Unexpected;** *Consultant in Disaster Response, and Speaker on Emergency Family Preparedness, History, Civil War, Flags, Korean War, etc. Community Education Officer (Retired Utah Dept. Pub. Safety), Radio Host KSUB, poet, and resident of Rockville, Utah.*

"After reading, pondering and re-reading many passages in this book, many memories are brought back to mind. Also an appreciation for those brave souls who battled the elements to eke out a living and raise a family in these trying circumstances.

I have been acquainted with many of the author's family which has been both delightful and rewarding.

. . .an easy reading book. I would recommend this book for [anyone] old, young and in between. "

—**F. Leon Lewis:** *Principal and Schoolteacher (Ret.) 31 yrs, Springdale, UT; Zion National Park Naturalist (Ret.) 14 yrs.; highly involved LDS member; a four-generations family man and husband (Warda Hirschi Lewis, 51 yrs). And you may have seen him with the Red Rock Rondo Band reciting his poetry.*

http://www.redrockrondo.com/whentheroostercrows.html

"It was wonderful to read Alaina's book. It brought [back] so many forgotten memories of my young years living on the ranch in south Texas. We didn't have any snow there, but living in the old drafty farm house with the wood cook stove always going, was a memory never to be forgotten.

Each morning the first chore was to get the stove going, then some chores getting the potatoes and onions from under the house. . . [the only cool spot to be found] . . . for the meals that day . . . it also built a self-reliant quality to our upbringing that made us . . . [have] respect for all.

Thanks for sharing your life with us Alaina, it re-kindles welcome memories of growing up and being responsible at an early age. "

—**Bill Curd,** EE *(Ret.)*

"I am reading it for the 2nd time now. It's a joy in the sense you covered it all, the highs and the lows of life. . .

Historical treasure . . .how grateful we can be now-a-days. How would we know our easy life today if there wasn't a comparison from personal experience?. . .the photos bring the story/events to life."

"I know what it is like to overcome childhood conditioning. Still working on . . .[overcoming] my black rocks. . .I receive courage from your pioneer book."

—**Karin B.**, *Arizona*

Comments from author's sister:

"This is a good read. . .

. . .Living through hard times made [us] appreciate the basic things of life. As she said, hot milk-toast tasted wonderful, It still tastes good to me, also.

I was born in 1933, late in the Depression, but our own family Depression lasted for a long time, until the ReHab loan was paid off. We still had a lot of fun as a family. We all loved it when Mom read aloud to us, even when we were older.

I remember hearing all about the old jail in the [back of the] bank [building] from someone who was part of the chicken stealing [and chicken] cooking group."

—Rhean Pendleton, *Pine Valley, UT*

Disclaimer: This is an historical narrative and a personal memoir based on my life, and the lives of others in my community—family, friends, ancestors, pioneers, and even roaming explorers. I have used real names sometimes, and omitted other names, as I deemed necessary to preserve the integrity and dignity of the townspeople. I have intended no harm. My purpose is only to show real people in real-life situations, to illustrate the times and what we went through to grow a community and make it through The Depression.

— *Alaina Newhart*

ISBN 978-0-615-42926-7

Library of Congress LCCN: 2011921862

2nd Printing 1112011 (ymountainpress.com)
3rd Printing 1242011 (mirasmart.com)

Back Cover Photo: April Neilson
Cover and Book Design: Merridy Jeffery

Contact Info: merridy@famlink.com
Merridy Jeffery

Merridy S. Jeffery
10897 Aspen Trail
Zeeland, MI 49464-8696

Black Rocks and Cold Wind

Surviving the Good Old Days

By

Alaina Newhart

To My BFF Karl,
Thank you for taking time
to get to know "elders".
Alaina
(& Merridy)

Black Rocks and Cold Wind

Surviving the Good Old Days

Table of Contents

Acknowledgments

In 1982 I took a creative writing class. The teacher, Rich Keller, assigned us to write about our most memorable experience. Glancing back I could not ignore the powerful impact of the Great Depression and the effects it had on every aspect of my life.

What I handed in was not much more than an essay. What emerged over the years is this expanded account, although I've saved my middle years for another book.

Thank you, Mr. Keller, for being interested in learning what life was like before you were born. Your favorable critique about my story greatly influenced me, and inspired me to continue writing.

The next time I took a writing class it was in Menlo Park, CA. I continued on with my story and was helped so much more by instructor Sheila Dunec and my classmates.

I am grateful to Merridy Jeffery, for her editorial insights, book design, word processing, image processing and for seeing this project through to the end. Many thanks to all my children who read it and made comments: Dinah Hamilton, April Neilson, Glenda Crapo, Wayne Neilson and Craig Neilson.

My cousin, Victor Hall, is a fine historian and has supplied many old photos, some of which are included. I also drew from Thelma Hall's family photo collection. Thank you both. Additional photos were obtained courtesy of the SUU, Sherratt Library, Special Collections Dept. Thank you, Paula Mitchell, for making these photos accessible.

This is my story as I remember it.

Foreword

Alaina [aka Glenna Hall] Newhart's book, *Black Rocks and Cold Wind* is a treasure chest of life in a small town in the American southwest in the early 20th century. I particularly like its subtitle, *Surviving the Good Old Days,* because her writing details the family life and social interactions in the Hurricane I'd heard of earlier from my mother, Elaine Hartley. Mother grew up there twelve years earlier with her three sisters and a younger brother, near the life-giving irrigation ditch. Alaina and her family, on the other hand, had to survive far from water near the volcanic basalt flow on the northwest side of town.

She movingly describes the adaptation of her family to hardship through hard work, innovation and sacrifice. Her dispassionate analysis of the interrelationships within her family is priceless. She explains how to build a 'refrigerator' for which no electricity is needed and how to plan and prepare meals when the larder is almost bare. Her story is replete with moving examples of the value in sharing of resources, labor and expertise between families in the community.

She revealed detail I'd not heard before on the entertaining subject of boys stealing watermelons and tipping over outhouses. It was a pleasant surprise to learn that she was a grade school classmate of my mother's youngest sibling Eldean.

This important book brings out details of the workings of society as it once was in rural America. I highly recommend it as a factual primer on human survival under difficult conditions—and equally for the sparkle and wit Alaina uses to describe that life so tenderly and so clearly.

—Wayne L. Hamilton, PhD., author of

The Sculpturing of Zion, Paragon Press.

Black Rocks and Cold Wind

Surviving the Good Old Days

Just as evening set in, first a flicker, then the struck match set the dry brush on fire. Moments later, the dried out old boards of the sheep shearing corral also caught on and the whole thing shot flames high into the sky. As soon as the fire got started, a young arsonist mounted his horse, and avoiding the main road where he might be spotted, followed a sheep trail to the steep hillside. He cautiously picked his way down the rocky incline over the crude and treacherous trail, heading as fast as he could to the safety of his home in Hurricane.

The largest sheep shearing corral in the west was located at the top of the ledges above Hurricane. This shearing operation provided jobs for several men and boys. For years, the sheep men and the cattle men were engaged in a battle for control of the range lands, although no shots were ever fired. This ongoing situation caused great aggravation to the cattle ranchers because the sheep ate the grass so close to the ground it left nothing for the cattle to feed on.

In desperation, someone had secretly hired the young man to get rid of the corral. When the corral was set ablaze, it was rumored that the cattlemen were responsible. I have been told who lit the match, but if asked, I will declare it to be only a rumor.

I remember many historical events from childhood, such as: Franklin Delano Roosevelt serving twelve years as President of the United States; the rise and fall of Adolf Hitler and other World War II events; and the passive resistance of Mahatma Gandhi. But the thing that drastically affected me was the "Crash of '29," and its consequences for several years to come. Virtually all of my formative years were spent in dealing with the hardships of "The Great Depression".

This is a story about people tackling a waterless land, with a desire to survive and grow a town.

Rockville

Reaching back into my genetic history, I'll begin with my Mormon pioneer grandparents—my father's folks—and how they came to be in Southern Utah, which resulted in my growing up in a rustic settlement just beginning to take shape as a civilized little town.

In the 1860's my great-grandparents had been somewhat comfortably settled in Salt Lake City when their church leader, Brigham Young, "called" them to leave their home, and with three or four children, move over two hundred miles south to help colonize a small valley already inhabited by a few families. The settlement was located a few miles downstream on the Virgin River from what is now Zion National Park.

It was Brigham Young's divine calling to scatter his faithful flock, sending them to remote areas where they could farm and establish new Mormon colonies. Being church business it did not matter that they were ill-prepared for such foolhardy ventures. In those hard times, obeying his counsel was certainly a test of faith in "*The Church*" and their devotion to him, their living prophet.

Loading a few necessities into a wagon box to be drawn by two work horses, took considerable planning. Figuring out what to take and what to leave behind was crucial. Grains, wheat, barley and corn, for food and for planting were most important. Cookware and other kitchen essentials were needed. All the quilts and clothing they owned were stuffed into the wagon. A couple of cows were tied to the back of the wagon to walk the distance. The family perched atop the load and set off on an arduous journey of two weeks duration over rough tracks.

At their new location, families helped each other build dwellings from rocks that had fallen down the steep hillside. They, of course, named the town Rockville. It's still on the map today. It's still a small town.

The first winter was extremely difficult, for the new arrivals, in keeping their children warm and fed. And the following years did not get much easier. Freezing and starvation were still a threat. Incidentally, Brigham Young was perhaps the original 'snowbird' wintering in St. George about fifty miles southwest of Rockville. St. George, settled a few years earlier and maintaining a mild winter climate later became known as Utah's “Dixie” probably because of its warmer climate, red dirt, and the fact that Brigham Young wanted the settlers to grow cotton. Although they endured many hardships during the cold winters in Rockville, the people were able to keep going in spite of the fact that families continued to grow in numbers of children. Mormon members did not question a church edict to multiply and replenish the earth. I'm sure this was a plan to increase the Mormon population.

Large families were strongly encouraged—never mind how the hapless parents were to feed, clothe and shelter their children. In 1950 I met a man who's story illustrates this.

Illustration 1: My grandparents, Alfred and Julia (Hansen) Hall with first five boys. Rockville, UT 1893. Alfred was born in Salt Lake in 1858. (Photo by Curtis, Salt Lake City, Courtesy Victor Hall)

It was winter and my husband and I, along with our three small children, were living in an old house in Grafton. It was the one right next to the much photographed church there in the center of town, and we were the final residents of what had already become a ghost town. Our normal house was a wind-whipped cabin out on the 'dry farm' near present day Apple Valley, east of Hurricane, and we were living in Grafton to escape the cold of our shack.

One day I saw an old man in the street and went out to talk to him. His name was Mr. Russell, and since I saw no means of transportation, I assumed he had walked down from Rockville, three or four miles to the east.

He indicated the crude house on the opposite side of the street and said it was the one he had lived in as a child. He was a very bitter man as he told me how his polygamous father had brought his mother and the children there to live, only to leave them and go back to Salt Lake to his other family. The father rarely came back to bring food and then, not nearly enough to last until his next visit. They didn't have enough wood to burn in the old adobe fireplace for warmth or for cooking, and they were severely short of blankets and clothing. Starving and cold, it is a wonder they survived. Even as an old man he remained resentful, and his impaired childhood had colored his life so much that he never married.

I realize his story was not the usual for pioneer families, but it is an indication of the hardships larger families endured. My grandparents, Alfred and Julia Hall, had nine children by the time their family was complete.

Since the Rockville community was within Utah Territory, the land was free, helping to expand the colonization of Mormons from Salt Lake, and the westward movement of settlers in general, who came west to seek new opportunities.

Utah Territory was created in 1850 and was carved into its final configuration as a state in 1896; portions having gone to Nevada Territory and what is now the southwest corner of Wyoming and western Colorado.

These poor pioneers did survive and were able to hang on for many winters, subsisting on what foods they could grow for themselves and their animals. Year after year, however, violent summer storms—cloud bursts producing flash floods—took a toll on their farms along the river.

My grandfather owned a farm where the lodge now stands in Zion National Park. That too, was being eroded. So much soil was washed away, literally taking the farm land, washing it downstream, that it became necessary to seek land elsewhere. After many meetings and much discussion, a few men went out on horseback to find suitable land for farming and big enough to accommodate more people.

A large, elevated mesa of many hundreds of acres, covered with sagebrush, rabbit brush, cactus and other drought hardy plants, was located fifteen miles from Rockville, downstream and to the west, on the opposite side of the Virgin River. The river cut a deep chasm through the Colorado Plateau and Zion, draining its waters to the west, eventually merging with the Colorado River.

Illustration 2: Hurricane Bench prior to settlement, 1903. Men are camping out and beginning to stake out farming plots. (Photo: Courtesy Victor Hall)

In order to settle this elevated bench, it was necessary to cross the river. The impossible part was that soon after leaving Rockville, the river ran into a canyon. Deeply carved into the sheer cliff walls of the limestone and basalt flow, it was about 200 feet deep at this point. There was absolutely no way to get the water out of the river and up onto that higher plateau.

However, there were men in the group who refused

to take “no” for an answer. My grandfather, Alfred Lorenzo Hall, was one of them. They even brought in a surveyor from St. George who was certain it *could not* be done.

The Virgin River was a comparatively small trickle as rivers go, but it was the life blood of these pioneers. Luckily there was a convenient break in the walls near the chosen land providing a passage for wagons. Fording the river was only possible at times of low water, and even so it was a very rocky and rough endeavor.

Illustration 3: Virgin River Canyon, looking west. Black dots show a proposed bridge just west of the hot springs (not shown). Look closer and you can see where the canal is carved into the hillside—a horizontal line along the upper left side of picture, with lighter rock 'tailings' below. You can see the original road just before bend in the river. Later, a bridge would span this canyon. The Hurricane “Bench” is the flat mesa in center . (Photo: Courtesy Victor Hall)

The approach down to the river on the north side was quite accessible, but getting up the precipitous south side was a real challenge. Trudging up the steep incline, the horses hooves as well as the wagon wheels slipped on cinder gravel as they climbed alongside a lava knoll. The local Paiute Indians called the area *Timpoweap*, "Rock Canyon."

In 1776, this crossing was used by explorer and missionary, Father Escalante. An interesting entry in his journal describes the Paiute Indians inhabiting the area just north of the river crossing near Toquerville. There were three small fields of corn planted and watered by irrigation ditches. In all his explorations, these were the only natives he had seen cultivating anything. His company of fourteen men spent a couple of days in the area where they received maize from the Indians (their staples were down to only two chunks of chocolate when they got here) and then, undoubtedly, they had a good soak in the hot springs that were located up-river from the crossing.

> *"We continued downstream toward the south, and having traveled half a league, we swung southwest, leaving the river, but a high cliff without any way to get down forced us to go back more than a quarter of a league and return to the river which here runs southwest. Two other small rivers join it here, one which comes from the north-northeast, and the other from the east. The latter consists in great part of hot and sulphurous water, and for this reason we named it Rio Sulfúreo. Here there is a beautiful grove of large black cottonwoods, some willows, and wild grape vines. In the stretch where we retraced our steps there are ash heaps, veins and other signs of minerals, and many stones of reddish mica. We crossed the Rio del Pilar and the Sulfúreo near the place where they join, then going south we ascended a low mesa between crags of shiny black rock."*
>
> — *Journal of Father Escalante* [Ref 4]

This mesa, later called the Hurricane Bench, was to become the new home for the settlers from Rockville.

Hurricane Canal 1893-1906

The Hurricane Canal Company, organized in 1893, was signed by fifty-three men. John Steele and James Jepson figured out that if they diverted the river upstream, it would be at a high enough elevation to flow onto the Hurricane bench. To do this, they needed a fifteen-foot-high dam, and a channel to run the water.

The men eagerly got started on this project which involved carving, chiseling, blasting and tunneling along the hillside, at times through solid rock. In places where this was impossible they built flumes of wood supported by tall trestles that skirted the cliff-side. After the first diversion dam washed out, they built another. It too failed against the raging waters. The third dam held.

The canal project was funded by the men. They made numerous trips to Salt Lake to procure blasting powder, and other needed supplies with the proceeds from wheat that was grown in Rockville. When they didn't have blasting powder, the procedure was to bake the rocks with a bonfire, and once heated, they would smash down with sledge hammers to break up the rocks. It was a long and grueling process. They lined the canal with clay which was tamped down, creating a seal. Discovering a band of lime in the hillside, they built a kiln to process it, and used it for making cement. The lime kiln can still be seen if you know where to look.

After World War II, the entire length of the canal was cemented, which was a feat in itself considering the canal was eight feet wide, by four feet deep, and when complete, ran seven and one half miles long.

As if the terrain wasn't enough of a challenge, if they were to survive, the summers needed to be devoted to farming, so most of the canal work had to be done in the

Illustration 4: Trailing along the hillside, the canal overlooks the Pah Tempe hot springs and that 'new' bridge which was previously only black dots. (Photo: Courtesy Victor Hall, Ref. 2, Sons of Utah Pioneers DVD)

winter months. As the years dragged on, fewer and fewer men showed up to help, and the money finally ran out. Quitting was unthinkable, so they were able to persuade the LDS Church in Salt Lake to invest in the project. That $5000 stock purchase made it possible to finish the job.

My grandfather, Alfred Hall, was one of the most persistent workers, as well as a significant financial supporter. He was a ruggedly handsome man, but was bossy and difficult to work with on the canal construction, challenging anyone who disagreed with him on the best way to proceed with the project.

Even though he donated cash and worked more hours than anyone else, because of his disposition, the others were reluctant to credit him publicly for his contributions. Determined to succeed, he also demanded that his older boys work on the canal almost beyond their endurance. The boys labored so arduously that one of them, Merrill, swore he never again wanted to see a wheelbarrow, and to his credit, throughout his life, he never owned one to use on his own farm.

Illustration 5: William Hinton on Hurricane canal. A bag over his shoulder contains the photographic equipment of R. D. Adams. As you can see, the steep hillside made this a very precarious place to work. (Photo: R.D. Adams, Courtesy SUU, Sherratt Library, Special Collections)

Although they were sorely challenged the men did not consider giving up. The pioneer spirit was to "press on". The main part of the canal took eleven grueling years to build by hand and hard labor. The water finally flowed onto the bench. Then it was another two years to complete all the lower channels and ditches. The Canal, carved from the side of the Hurricane Cliffs formation, is listed in the National Historic Register.

The canal was used for irrigation until the Quail Lake Project (1980's) was built, but remains valuable still for managing flood control.

Hurricane Bench

Since Utah had recently become a state, the settlers were now required to purchase this new land they would migrate to. They'd need enough for building houses and farming. The state now made this land available at a dollar and twenty-five cents per acre. Before the canal was finished a few families had moved onto the land. They lived in tents, dugouts, wagon boxes, and lean-to's made of cedar poles and bark.

They hauled water in wooden barrels up from the river. Back from the rugged trek, after the jostling stopped, the sand and dirt settled to the bottom of the barrels providing acceptable drinking water for both people and animals. These trips to haul water were timed according to the weather, between storms, to avoid water that was too muddied by runoff. Eventually they were able to travel a few miles to the north, beyond a small village called Toquerville—named after an Indian Chief—to get pure water from a good spring.

To prepare for the completion of the canal, the men dug irrigation ditches. Digging with only shovels and muscle power, they channeled the land. The ditches extended several miles each way, crisscrossing the breadth and length of the mesa, all networked up to where the canal would enter from the hillside on the east. The term “ditch digger” is often considered the lowest of the low today; that being a most humble predicament to be found in. But preparing the expanse for irrigation called on its elite men to skillfully dig the ditches. They were a proud people who demanded top-of-the-line ditches. They were flawless. No one shirked. Excitement and exultation knew no bounds when the head-gate was lifted and water gushed down the canal filling the ditches—changing the value of the land forever.

Although irrigation ditches were being dug and men were camping out, farming their new land during the week then returning to Toquerville, Rockville, and Virgin on the weekends, it would take another two years to see actual residents on the Hurricane bench. The Thomas M. Hinton family were the first full-time settlers in 1906. That year would see another ten rooftops appear. 1907 brought sixteen more families. In 1909 another twelve families took up residence, including my grandparents.

Illustration 6: Hurricane,1906 barns and houses beginning to appear. Note the canal in the foreground and along foothills. First full-time settler was Thomas M. Hinton. He and his family were allowed to live in a barn/granary he was building for someone else. (Photo: Wm. L. Crawford, Courtesy Victor Hall)

The families who originally settled Rockville, loaded their few possessions into wagons, hitched up their teams of horses and rumbled the fifteen miles down the rocky road to start all over again. They arrived on the land to renew pioneering skills learned only a few short years earlier in Rockville. Once again they would carve out a living on barren land with nothing but a few crude tools and themselves to rely on.

The town fathers plotted out the land in blocks, with parcels of eight to a mile. Each block was divided into four lots, allowing plenty of space for family gardens, orchards, and domestic animals. With houses being built, the next step was to dig cisterns for the household water supply. Some were round. Some square. They were usually about twelve feet deep and perhaps twelve feet across. When possible, they were cemented then filled with ditch water. As usual, when the sediment settled, water could be hauled up with a bucket on a rope for culinary use. Beyond the town area, twenty-acre plots were allocated for individually owned farms.

Settling In

Almost without exception, those who were part of the exodus from Rockville were, of necessity, tough people with harsh personalities. Raw survival took precedence over niceties. Getting along peaceably with each other, however, was primary. They helped each other when anyone was in need. The women never hesitated to sit up all night with a mother who had sick children, offering folk remedies or just emotional support. The women always brought prepared food whenever a neighbor was coping with trouble, or illness, or a death in the family. The men loaned their farm tools to each other and helped repair often broken implements. This included anything from sharpening tools, shovels and plows, to binding broken handles together with baling wire. Men bringing baling wire were as essential as women bringing food in those days.

Once in the valley, they immediately set about tilling the soil—the hard way. A common sight was a man with the horse's reins looped over his head, across one shoulder, and under the arm guiding the blade of the plow by its two wooden handles.

They sowed seeds into the parched ground and

gratefully ran the ditch water down the rows expecting the seeds to germinate and grow. Watering was done according to “turns”. No one dared touch a drop when it wasn't his irrigation turn. Many years later a man was killed on the ditch bank during a shovel fight as he was accused of stealing water from a neighbor when it was not his turn.

From what I’ve read or heard, every great city began on the banks of a sizable river or lake. Or at least a spring or watering hole of some sort. These pioneers in Southern Utah at the turn of the twentieth century saw nothing but desert terrain—barren ground dotted with sagebrush, prickly pear cactus, rabbit brush, and lizards—and a ragged, but sometimes temperamental, little muddy stream seemingly out of their reach. And yet, they had a dogged determination to get some land on which to live and farm. And they even figured out how to get river water up on the bench to tame the land for their use.

Therefore Hurricane, as it was later named, was never destined to become a great city. It is just now, a hundred years later, bursting at its seams with over 13,000 inhabitants. In 1906, the town was literally started 'from scratch’ by a bunch of desperate, determined people needing a home. They had no choice but to make it work.

Hurricane farms would eventually boast fields of alfalfa, watermelons, sugar cane, various grains, vineyards, and very fine orchards of peaches, cherries, pecans, and walnuts, to name a few.

Lumber Mill

Forging ahead with their minds set on establishing a sound community, some of the men constructed a lumber mill. Out east of town, is the Kaibab Plateau formation, which consists of several stepped up layers, (or stepped down, and to the south, it ends in the Grand Canyon). On a much higher plateau, two levels up from Hurricane, is a sizable mesa with tall pine and cedar trees.

To access this lumber, it was necessary to get up to the higher level. A steep hill, now known as the Hurricane Cliffs Formation, reared up along the east side of the bench. The men had built a dug-way up the hill that was so rugged, one wonders how they were able to build it, not to mention expecting their horses to pull wagons up it. Many years later, when we used that road going up to our dry farm—it was not irrigated—we trudged up the hill on foot so as not to demand too much from our horses pulling the wagon.

After that initial hill climb, the men found a way to get to the top of the timbered mountain, perhaps another thousand feet higher up, where they chopped down the trees using only the tools of the day—long-handled axes and crude hand saws. Up there, they sawed the lumber, bound the planks into bundles to minimize damage, and dropped them over the edge of the sheer cliff to land several hundred feet below on a sandy area. This was known as the Canaan Mountain lumber drop. The saw mill was run by horse power—real horse power.

At the bottom of the drop the planks were loaded onto horse-drawn wagons and hauled back down to the lower level to town. It took many trips to fetch enough lumber even for a small house. The horses could pull only so much weight and the wagons size was limited, as was the man-power to saw the lumber.

A similar mill was located a few miles to the north in what is now Zion National Park near the Weeping Rock. This lumber drop was much more of a challenge. David Flanigan devised a framework to lower the lumber over the edge using a cable system, where it was required to descend 2000 feet. It is interesting that he had first conceived the idea when still a teenager, in 1885, but he had to wait sixteen years until he could put his dream into action. When his dog was the first to give it a test ride in 1901, it was "real scart" according to David's brother William, who documented the event in his journal. If you know where to look, the framework can still be seen today. It's still called Cable Mountain.

Illustration 7: Jim Crawford at top of Cable Mountain Lumber Drop site, looking down into Zion, 2000 feet to the valley floor. (Photo: Wm. L . Crawford from a stereopticon slide. Courtesy Victor Hall)

What's in a Name?

The town's being named Hurricane, was no misnomer, given the fierce wind which always blew in the winter time coming from the northeast off Smith's Mesa and northwest off the snow-covered peaks of Pine Valley Mountain.

Erastus Snow and another man from St. George were stopped atop the hill getting ready to start down the steep, fearsome grade into the settlement. A vicious north wind buffeted them, shaking their confidence and the horse-drawn buggy as they checked the brakes. The horses too, were irritated at the wind whipping and whooshing their forelocks and grit into their eyes. They shook their heads and pranced impatiently, making it difficult for the drivers to control them. Then a sudden blast hit them, lifted the white canvas cover off the buggy, and sailed it away. Erastus exclaimed, "*by gab, what a HURRICANE !*" The name stuck.

The Fort

In the 1850's, long before the Hurricane mesa was settled, cattlemen from Toquerville were ranging cows in this area. They were being plagued with Indian raids and found it necessary to round up the cattle and horses at night to protect the livestock from these marauding Indians. In the 1860's, the men built a simple rock fort and a large rock corral. Two sentries would stand guard during the night. If the animals became restless it was likely they were being stalked. At the first sign of animals stirring, the watchmen were to set a fire to signal the ranchers to the north, in Toquerville about three miles (as-the-crow-flies) and across the river, six miles by horseback. The cowboys would need to ride hard to get there in time to save the animals.

Incidentally, in those days animals were branded by searing their flanks with red-hot irons marking the owner's logo or initials. Nowadays, I've seen animals simply marked with spray paint. The plight of animals has *certainly* improved.

Illustration 8: Hirschi Brothers branding cattle in Rockville. (Photo: Wm L. Crawford, Courtesy SUU Sherratt Library, Special Collections)

The fort was situated on a little pointy hill at the north end of the bench. It was constructed by stacking black lava rocks into walls about twenty feet long, by twenty feet wide and six feet high. A foot-high slot on each side allowed the 'look-out' to scan for animal unrest or to poke a rifle barrel through. Extending from the fort, they made a sizable oblong corral, about 210 feet by 230 feet, also using lava rocks. Although rocks were in abundance, the walls were only three feet high—sufficient to contain the animals.

As a teenager, I used to walk up on the hill about a half mile from our house to visit the remains of the fort. Some of the rocks had toppled off but the main walls were still there. The corral walls had mostly fallen.

I would sit on a rock in the sunshine and think about the Indian conflicts and how it all had changed. By this time, Indians were coming to our house and holding out a dirty cloth gunny sack indicating my mother was to put food in it. Flour or wheat was about all we could spare. They too were being affected by the white man's economy.

Strangely enough, after all the work of building the fort, it was only used for a signal fire one time! That was

Illustration 9: Ruins of the Rock Fort constructed in the 1860's by cowboys from Toquerville. (Photo: Glenda Crapo)

the work of a young guard, Tommy Willis, who wanted to know just how long it would actually take the men to get to the fort. The first Hurricane area prankster.

Today, what remains of the fort is fenced in and designated as a monument. My brother, Roland Hall, was instrumental in creating this monument, along with many others, who supported the project, restored the walls, and

Illustration 10: Rock Fort Monument, established 2002. (Photo: Glenda Crapo)

built the monument. Lane Blackmore graciously donated the land.

The town has expanded in all directions. An athletic field is nearby the fort. A block to the west, the road heads north, down into the canyon and to the original river crossing.

Alvin Meets Ann

Illustration 11: Alvin Hall, my father. (Photo: Courtesy Thelma Hall)

My father was eighteen when his parents, Alfred and Julia Hall, moved the family to Hurricane. He had gotten his grade school education in a one-room-schoolhouse in Rockville so he was ready to travel to St. George to begin 9th grade, eventually to complete high school there. Alvin and his cousin, Orson Hall, rode horses the eighteen-mile distance on week-ends, and rented a room during the week. A few miles to the west of Hurricane, the Virgin River curved to the south where the banks were flat enough for horses to cross, making it possible to get to St. George.

It was in St. George where my father met Ann Pickett and convinced her to marry him. Ann was a shy, pretty girl who knew nothing about dating. She had fallen down when she was sixteen and threw her knee out of place. Therefore she could not walk to school and didn't finish high school. She was very bright, however, and picked up all kinds of information which came across as her seeming to be well-educated.

Ann's father, Horatio Pickett, had been married and had a grown family of six, when his wife died. He then married his oldest daughter's girlfriend, my grandmother, Philena Hunt. Ann was second from oldest of this second family of five children. Grandpa Pickett was an intelligent, well-educated man who was a lawyer. He owned the mortuary, an unpainted board, warehouse-type structure under large mulberry trees in the backyard. On his

Illustration12: Young ladies of St. George. Sewing bee. My mother, Ann, seated, far right. Her younger sister, LaVern, in front. (Courtesy Thelma Hall)

mothers side, he had a rich history, going back to the martyr John Rogers, of 1555 fame. Horatio was a carpenter, cabinet maker, choir master, rock quarry man, a librarian, a politician, one of the organizers of the St. George Builders Union, and was a planing mill operator, etc. An energetic man, he also became president of the newly built Mormon Temple in St. George.

It is rumored that my dad liked to talk with Grandpa Pickett so much, that that's the real reason he spent a lot of time visiting at the Pickett house, not necessarily to call on Ann. It's not surprising that they scarcely knew each other when they got married, in the Temple, of course.

Illustration 13: My mother, Ann Pickett, about 1916, St. George, UT. (Photo: Courtesy Thelma Hall)

Imagine my mother's surprise when she moved to Hurricane only to find it was still in its beginning stages. In effect, my parents were second genera-tion pioneers who helped to settle this town.

The younger children of early settlers attended school in private homes. Church was also held in members' homes. In 1908, Graff's Mercantile was built, and a post office was operated out of a private home. A few years later the town boasted an actual church house and a school house, bringing the ninth grade back from St. George. Anyone attending college went to St. George.

The church house lasted until the 1980's when it was deemed unsound and was torn down. The spot has been converted into a park named Heritage Square, where stands a monument to the founders. My father donated an Indian tomahawk for the monument. It was a black stone which he found on Little Creek Mountain when he was gathering a load of wood. The monument builders cemented it into the structure, and later someone had apparently admired it so much that they chipped it out and stole it. There is also a memorial to World War II veterans listing each by name. The old library still stands on the west side of the square and has been converted to a museum.

In 1909, when my grandparents arrived, there was a census of 336 residents.

Illustration 14: Hurricane, 1910. Every year they took a picture of the town and updated the list of families who arrived. Notice cleared farming plots becoming evident. (Photo: Wm. L. Crawford, Courtesy Victor Hall)

In 1910, another fourteen families came, and each year there was a photograph taken of the growing town with a listing of the new families.

In 1913, the town gained a doctor, Dr. Wilkinson.

In 1914, Charles Petty built a 'show house'. The movies were run by a gas-powered movie projector and sometimes the film caught fire. Its generator was blaringly loud and that proved to be the only advertising needed to attract the residents. When we heard that generator, we begged our dad for a nickel to go to the show. As coins were scarce in our family, it was rare that any of us got to go. Until the late 1980's the movie house was a fixture on Main Street with its wooden floors that squeaked. Of course, the projector had been updated, but whenever my grown kids came to town, they thought it was a real treat to go see a movie, even though the ticket price had been raised to a dollar and fifty cents.

My father graduated high school in St. George in 1916. He married Ann in 1917.

By 1917, in just a few short years, Hurricane went from a standing start to being a growing, prospering, and functioning town. Pure water had been piped in from the spring north of Toquerville, perhaps a distance of eight rugged miles, including crossing the Virgin River. Electricity had been brought in and later, the telephone was introduced, although only a handful of townsfolk could afford one.

Illustration 15: Hurricane, 1915. The canal water begins to change the landscape forever. (Photo: J.J. Booth, Courtesy Victor Hall)

There were now one-hundred families and eight-hundred residents. These people were still very resourceful. They always found a way to get things done.

The mercantile, established in 1908 by Charles and Frank Petty, and Melbourne DeMille was a great success and served as a social hub of sorts, being in the center of it all, at the corner of State Street and Main Street. DeMille sold out by 1913 and the Petty's sold to E.J. Graff in 1928, who named it Graff's Mercantile. Graff's was tradition. You could buy every-thing from shoes, overalls, knitting needles and hardware in the front, and in the back was the grocery section. This building still stands and is still in use, although recently it has been sub-divided for smaller businesses. It still has the creaky wooden floors and friendly store owners.

Across the street to the south of Graff's, was the gas station, the new bank, and the meat market, sharing a run-on building.

By the time I was born in 1924, Hurricane was a well-established, thriving, farming community.

Businesses thrived as did fruit orchards and vegetable farms. All householders, to some degree, were earning a living. Some of the men owned sheep and cattle herds, which caused much rivalry as the sheep ate the range grasses to the ground, leaving no good areas on the hillsides to graze the cattle[1].

1*Editorial Note: Not surprisingly, the sheep conflict was the primary bone of contention with the Paiute Indians in the Rockville and Grafton areas before people moved from there. The Natives had been friendly to the settlers, helping them out in many ways until they discovered just how destructive the sheep were to the land. Suddenly there was competition for their food resources.*

Illustration 16: In just a few short years, Hurricane became a very nice farming community . 1929 (Photo: Courtesy Victor Hall.)

A few prospering citizens built substantial houses with bricks and good lumber.

The Hastings family in Virgin, who lived in a dugout, (imagine a mostly submerged house in a hillside), were able to better their circumstances by purchasing land in Hurricane and building a house. Mr. Hastings' mother, a widow, had been blind for many years and refused to leave her dugout home because she was comfortable knowing where everything was located. To accommodate his mother, he built an exact replica of her rooms on the side of the new house, duplicating everything to the last detail. She was then able to move into her new house without fear.

My grandfather's house was made of good quality lumber and had fancy curlicues across the top of the porch. This house also had transoms above the doors for fresh air ventilation between rooms. The house was yellow with white trim. Pretty fancy. It has recently been torn down and a modern house has been built on the spot. Getting this house put up was not an easy task.

In midwinter, 1908, Grandpa and his sons, Lafe, Merrill, and my dad, Alvin, took two horse teams and wagons to Orderville about fifty miles away (on the map it's north east of Zion Park) to get lumber for building his new house in Hurricane. Grandpa's brother-in-law, John Stout, owned the mill and had set aside lumber for them.

On the way out to the mill one of the horses foundered. It had eaten too much of something, perhaps wheat, and had filled up with gas. If not taken care of, the horse was bound to die. Grandpa knew the right procedure and thrust a knife into the horse in just the perfect place to relieve the gas, saving its life.

Coming back, as they reached the Coral Pink Sand Dunes, the horses could not pull their loads through the sand. With typical pioneer ingenuity they double-teamed one wagon dragging it across the sand, then took the four horses back to retrieve the other wagon.

Their circuitous route took them around the fringes of high mountains going southwest then northwest back toward Hurricane. Many miles later they reached what was known as the Big Plains, twelve miles from their destination. They had been suffering all day through cold wind when, late in the day, a ferocious, blinding blizzard struck. The two coats each wore were not nearly enough to keep them warm. On the way out they had stashed some hay at Big Plains, planning to camp there. But now the hay was missing. Someone had discovered it and helped themselves. Since the horses must be fed, they had no choice but to leave the wagons—loaded with their precious lumber—and ride the horses home.

Illustration 17: Alfred Hall house, about 1917. (Photo: Courtesy Victor Hall)

The blizzard was still raging and by now their ears were frozen and their hands were so stiff they could barely unhitch the harnesses from the wagon tongues.

Grandpa and Lafe, took one team and headed north down rugged canyons seeking the comfort of home. It was so dark the horses were allowed to sense their way around boulders and drop-offs. After seven miles or so, they eventually reached the river and crossed near the small town of Grafton. Turning east toward Rockville, the anxious horses hurried the last two or three miles, arriving home near midnight.

The other two horses had been borrowed from Grandma's brother in Hurricane, fifteen miles distant, so Merrill and Alvin headed west and eventually had to descend the steep grade into Hurricane to return them. This road was not easy in the daytime and treacherous in the dark. Their ordeal was not finished. Before they could return the horses to their owners, it was necessary to continue two more miles on down to the river to water them. It was after midnight when they got the horses put safely back in their own corral.

Exhausted, the boys made their way to their future home site where their dad had built a granary. They slept inside, too cold and tired to eat any 'grub' from their saddle bags. What a way to spend Christmas Eve.

Daily Life

After a few years of grim hardship, most of the townspeople were having success in growing crops on the Hurricane land. They grew several kinds of grain, including barley, rye, and wheat plus vegetables, and dry beans, as well as fruit trees that were producing peaches, pears, cherries, apricots, and plums. They also grew pecan, walnut, and almond trees.

Jepson's had an almond orchard and I remember the whole neighborhood going there for an "almond husking bee". The men beat the the tree limbs with long poles, as well as climbed the trees to knock down the almonds. They gathered the nuts for the women and children to shuck.

The women and children pulled the rough, fuzzy outside husks off and sorted the nuts into bushel baskets. The husks went on the ground for the Jepson kids to clean up later. These were used to burn in the cook stove for fuel. We did this husking on shares. I don't remember the ratio, but it might have been two-thirds of the almonds to the owners and one-third to the shuckers. We took food any way we could get it.

I remember the youngest Jepson child, a boy four or five years old, was left unattended and unnoticed amongst the workers. With a rock, he cracked open almonds and ate them. They were not ripe enough to eat. Before the day was over the child began having convulsions. His brain, as well as his body, was damaged and he spent the rest of his life in a personal care center in northern Utah. Almonds contain cyanide. In fact in the United States, it is illegal to sell raw almonds unless they are heat-treated to remove the poisons.[2] Incidentally, in recent times, I heard

2 See bibliography reference 8.

of a young girl who ate too many green apples and died of it. And now, I also remember hearing about a herd of cattle that died after eating potatoes the farmer had dumped in their pasture; the potatoes had all turned green from the sunlight.

Now that survival seemed more certain, hardships were falling away and people were having an easier time of it. Personalities developed and a new joviality was beginning to surface.

My grandfather contributed his own brand of humor. Not intentionally. Originally, he had brought cash with him from Salt Lake and continued to increase it through business dealings. So in the 1920's he owned one of the few cars in town.

The introduction of cars necessitated a gas pump and a mechanic. All the dirt roads in town were lined on both sides with irrigation ditches.

My grandfather still retained his horse-riding mentality and drove his Model A Ford wildly around town—wherever he could ride a horse. He went through ditches and over rocky places and refused to give pedestrians their right-of-way, even when they were walking on the dirt 'sidewalk'. People were also accustomed to walking in the streets. But, when they heard the clattering noise of Grandpa's Ford coming, wherever they were, they scurried running for cover. Grandma Julia, sitting beside him clutching the window ledge to hang on, showed caring and compassion for others. When approaching pedestrians, she would invariably holler, "Alfred look out for those people!" Grandpa roared: "Down 'em. Let 'em git out of the way!" *Down* was his swear word. Being a religious man (I use that term loosely), that was the closest he could come to damning someone to hell. Being coarse, aggressive, and a domineering old coot, seemed not to detract from his churchiness. Often, he'd blast his horn at pedestrians: *Ah-OOO-Gah!*

When grandpa bought the car he cleared a parking space in the barn for it. The first time he drove in to park, the car kept going. He drove on out through the back wall shattering a big section, all the while yelling, *"Whoa! Whoa!"* while frantically yanking back on the steering wheel.

Expanding Family

My parents had begun their family right away. For at least eight years they lived with my father's parents. I was almost two when they were finally able to buy a two-room house five blocks away, which exceedingly pleased my mother. We referred to this house as the "Karl Roundy" house.

I had two older brothers and a sister. I was a year-and-a-half old when the next boy was born. This baby was a shock to me as I was used to being everyone's pride and joy. The boys chucked me under the chin saying "booty Glenna." With the new baby, suddenly it was over for me. It was February and the north wind was sifting in through the cracks around the windows. I remember being abandoned on a big bed over in the corner with a wet diaper. Mother sat in the rocking chair by the little wood-burning stove holding her new baby. The rest of the family were gathered around her. I had been replaced.

At this time my father earned a living working for Grandpa on the farm and running cattle on Crystal Ranch up on Kolob Mountain west of Zion. Grandfather's aim was to keep all six boys under his control. He paid them with farm products and barely enough cash to pay their utilities and buy an occasional pair of shoes for the kids. The boys were under bondage to the point that they couldn't afford to go and look for a better job.

In 1926, my father was somehow able to get a building loan for a house that would accommodate our growing family. The site, acquired from Grandpa, was a mile west of the center of town and sat on a hard-scrabble lava bed with almost no soil on it—not enough for gardening, at least that was my father's excuse for not growing food for his family. He preferred working for others in exchange for produce.

Building a house was a slow, arduous process—far removed from constructing with the labor-saving tools of today. There weren't any power tools in early day Hurricane. All lumber was sawed by hand. Before even starting the foundation of lava rocks, you had to first make a cement trough; a heavy-planked box with low sides. And, you couldn't just go buy a bag of sand to mix in. You next made a sand-box; a wooden platform with short sides to hold the sand. On one end was an upright board about two feet high, with a screen stretched from the top of this board at a ninety degree angle and attached to the other side of the platform. You then shoveled the coarse sand through the screen to sort out the finer particles. Then water, cement and sand were measured into the wooden trough and stirred with a big hoe that had holes in it. Scraping the hoe back and forth, you mixed until it was perfectly smooth and of the right consistency. Mixing cement all day was a sure way to develop some fine muscles.

Quite often we walked out to the site while the house was under construction, mother pushing the wicker baby buggy while we kids trailed along, the older ones running ahead. This was a very exciting excursion for us. Although small by any standards, this new house was many times larger than the two rooms we were currently crammed into.

After a year the new house was put together enough

for us to move in. Unable to contain our excitement, the first thing we children did was to try out all that space by running through the rooms until our parents, not amused, screeched us to a halt. This house was wooden frame with the outsides built of ship-lap lumber. It was painted immediately to preserve the wood, white with dark green trim. The inside walls and ceiling were covered with "Celotex," a cheaply made processed fiber material.[3] It didn't take much to poke a hole in the wall with an elbow or a foot. My brother, Gerald, was in the attic one day and accidentally stepped off a rafter. He fell through to the pantry floor shattering fruit bottles. Fortunately he was not hurt.

Our two bedrooms were connected by a walk-through closet. The doors did not have regular door knobs, just little snap latches that opened only from the outsides. One time when my parents were away, all of us kids plus a neighbor girl locked ourselves in this closet. It was totally dark inside. We were scared. We yelled for help but the nearest neighbor was half a block away. It was the mischievous neighbor girl who had pulled the door shut. The two older boys, Wendell and Gerald, kept ramming their weight against one of the doors until they broke the latch. To this day I shy away from dark closets with no two-way door knobs, or I prop the door open in case it might somehow lock itself.

Our new house felt so grand because it had a living room, kitchen, two bedrooms a bathroom, and a closet! As yet, no water connected to the bathroom, and heaven forbid, no water heater. The only water we had was from a tap over the kitchen sink. It was supplied from a cistern up a hilly slope from the house.

---

3 *Editorial note: The Celotex Company manufactured many insulation products which contained asbestos from the Carey mines in Canada. Sold from 1906 until 1973, it is surprising that their sales network reached miniscule population areas in Southern Utah in the 1920's and 1930's.*

Our cistern sat on an incline about fifty feet to the north of the house. The outlet pipe was about six inches from the bottom, allowing for the dirt to settle so relatively clean water could flow to the house. When it was our turn for irrigation water, the cistern was filled with ditch water and we drank this water after it settled. (Typhoid fever had not been invented yet.)

Illustration 18: This is what remains of our cistern, cement wall ruins. It is approximately located at 700 West 100 North. (Photo: Alaina Newhart)

There was a good board top on the cistern with an opening in the southeast corner, perhaps two feet square. This was to provide access for putting a ladder in when it was necessary to clean the sludge from the bottom. A wood-framed screen wire fit over the opening to protect it from animals. I remember climbing up the ladder and looking down into the water. A dead lizard was floating there. How could I forget a thing like that? I reported it and my father fished it out and tightened the lid more securely.

My Uncle Merrill dug his cistern close to their house. They used a tin bucket with a rope tied to the handle to hoist the water up. The walls and bottom were cemented. Like all the other cisterns in town, it was about twelve feet in diameter and close to twelve feet deep. It was covered with rough boards and had a separate wooden lid which was moved aside to accommodate the water bucket. After culinary water was piped in, they discontinued using it. Two years later Aunt Annabelle's sister and her children were visiting from Rockville. During the hot summer afternoon she lay down and took a nap. Suddenly she reared up on the bed and said with stark conviction, "Moral's drowned!" A mother's bond with her child had awakened her. Her four-year-old son had pried off the lid to the cistern and toppled in. Uncle Merrill had intended to bail the water out but just hadn't gotten around to it.

The city water line carrying spring water from Toquerville did not reach all the way out our street, or we could not afford to hook onto it, I don't remember which it was, but nonetheless we continued on with our cistern.

Our house also had a back porch niched into the northwest corner. It was boarded up about three feet then screened on up to the roof. When the boys got a little older, s teenagers, they slept on the porch—even in winter weather with the infamous fierce north winds howling. Heavy denim quilts helped, and my parents tacked up cardboard to keep it a little warmer. It was assumed boys were tougher than girls.

We slept on makeshift mattresses called 'straw ticks'. The outside casing was made of sturdy, heavy 'ticking' material of blue and white stripes. Straw was stuffed into it until it was full, then the opening was sewn shut across the end. Simple as that. Eventually the straw matted down, so we'd take the quilts off and vigorously shake the 'mattress' plumping it up again. After a few plumpings it was a goner so the straw had to be replaced.

Our wire-strung beds had iron legs and frames. Very strong wires were hooked to the rectangular frame on all sides, and where each wire intersected with another, they were hooked together with short wires. Three kids to a bed was the norm. The bed I shared with my sisters had a little give making me wonder if there were a lot of short wires not connected. It sagged in the middle. The middle kid usually complained of the others rolling into her, crowding. When fresh straw wasn't available, we just had to sleep on what was left of the mattresses, imprinting our bodies from the wires underneath.

Even though we had moved in, workmen still came to hang doors and lay linoleum in the kitchen. Some of the finer details were unfinished when the money suddenly ran out and we never did get the other floors covered. As a result, we often got splinters in our toes. We had no tweezers so mother had to dig them out with a needle. Then the toe would be wrapped in a rag—as white as we could find—a cheap version *Band-Aid*. We were grateful nonetheless, to finally be enjoying the comforts of our new house.

There was not much furniture. None in the living room except mother's foot-pumped organ that she had brought with her from St. George when she got married. We had a long, brown, rectangular drop-leaf, table in the kitchen. We ate our meals around it, but the idea of 'dining table' was not in our vocabulary. That concept was too fancy for us. It was referred to as the Grandpa Hall table. It had accommodated Grandpa's large family and now he had given it to us because our family was the largest of any of his children. Johnny Crawford had made it for him from Zions Cable Mountain lumber. It was a wonderful table. I have since learned the style is called *gate-leg* as my daughter bought one at an antiques shop in Colorado a few years back. Our chairs were a mix and match hodge-podge of whatever had been given to us, and we also used two long benches my dad had made.

The house was definitely a major improvement to our living situation, but still, we barely had enough money to scrape by. Father worked for people in exchange for fruits and vegetables and traded wheat he grew on his father's farm for flour from the flour mill. We also got credit at the store by trading the wheat and occasionally meat from our cows.

The Crash of 1929

About this time, the notorious "Crash of '29" hit.

Although the townspeople were well acquainted with scarcity, they were not prepared for the economy to suddenly collapse, plunging them into The Great Depression. It shattered their hard-earned confidence as many necessities of life were snatched away. Many folks had been able to move up enough to be comfortable and demonstrate a sense of security. Security gained through determination and struggle.

The proverbial rug was jerked out from under them. Everything seemed to stop in its tracks. Food, household goods and building supplies were accessible one day, and off limits the next. For those more secure, their sense of well-being tapered to a halt more gradually.

Until Black Friday, the onset of the Crash of '29, the economy had mostly been based on borrowed money. Credit had been so good that people had gone in debt for building decent houses (such as ours), for financing cattle herds and for sheep ranches. My dad had even borrowed money to buy a goat herd. Some farmers had taken out loans to tide them over until their orchards would produce the following summer. They had a good market for fruit in the surrounding towns, but sometimes the blossoms would get frozen in early spring leaving them with no crop at all. Farming—always a gamble.

The economy that had supported our little town turned a page into destitution. Curiously, our small local bank, with my grandfather a major stockholder, remained open throughout the Depression.

Being a child of five, I was not aware of the enormity of what was happening, but the mood in my family had changed from ordinary daily life to something tight-faced and grim. I did start getting the picture as our food supply dwindled and we were warned, as the main dish was passed around the table, "don't take so many potatoes," and "go easy on the gravy, that's all there is." It's not as though the food we previously had was more high class—usually just consisting of beans and potatoes—it's just that we were having less of it. Being a sensitive child, I felt guilty for taking my share of *whatever* we had. Potatoes and onions were the extent of our vegetables. We rarely had other vegetables as nothing would grow on our rocky soil. I yearned for carrots.

Our family was already accustomed to living stringently, and we continued to do so. If I was experiencing being more deprived, I was ignorant of it. My parents still bickered. We kids still fought. The bigger kids lording it over everyone who was smaller. So what was new at our house?

As to our circumstances, pre-Depression and Depression were about the same for us. In time, we got ground down to where there *was* a real difference. The change in my parents did not escape me. Daily life became more tinged with tension and short tempers. Worrying about paying off the house loan must have been terrible for them.

My father still got a few odd jobs now and then to keep us going. For some reason he was not working for his father on the farm nor managing the cattle. I remember Grandpa Hall as being an old man. Perhaps he had liquidated, but being a stern, uncharitable person, my father got no help from him. Due to other people's cash flow problems, there were fewer people hiring. As all crops were seasonal, there just wasn't much available. We did, however, usually hold over some wheat from the last years crop. It was always good for trading.

On occasion, my dad would borrow a team of horses and a wagon from his father to haul wood from the mountain. The closest tree range was 15 miles away. The wood was necessary to heat the stove for cooking and for keeping us warm in the winter. And it certainly roasted us when cooking food in the summer months. In summer, sometimes the stove was put outside for cooking and bottling fruit. All wood was chopped with an ax. People nowadays can't even understand the concept of chopping down trees with a simple ax. As you can imagine, the ax needed frequent sharpening with a whet stone.

With the load of wood coming down the steep hill into Hurricane, it was tricky to brake enough so as not to let the heavy load push against the horses. My dad was perched on the load as he drove through town and out to our place.

Our deficient cash-flow became almost non-existent. We barely existed in those years of depression as there was virtually no cash to be had. It literally dwindled down to nothing. I modify that slightly as I remember my mother once tell a salesman, "we've had less than $200 cash in this past year."

Occasionally a hungry man would walk into town looking for work and was willing to chop an armload of wood for something to eat. Even with our large family and dire circumstances, my mother was always there to help these people.

We were fortunate in that we lived in a small town among people who raised some varieties of produce. My father's excuse for not growing anything was we had no place to grow a garden. I'm wondering if he just didn't have a green thumb. There must have been a little bit of dirt on that lava-strewn two acres!

Dad worked for others in trade for potatoes, onions,

dry beans and flour from the flour mill, which was situated up against the Hurricane Hill by the canal. It was never enough to satisfy our hunger as we only had small amounts doled out to us. I guess the real issue was that our nutritional needs were not being met. I do not recall any over-weight kids in those days—certainly not in our family!

Breakfast was a sure thing. My mother soaked wheat during the night and next morning she cooked it until tender. It was served with milk or cream. We always had a cow and someone to milk it. The girls in the family were spared that job. When we were small we sometimes took our tin cups out for dad to squirt milk in, directly from the cow. The milk was warm and tasted good.

We always had whole wheat bread—not fancy but nutritious and filling. Often our meal was bread and milk gravy, made by browning flour in the frying pan then gradually stirring in the milk to thicken, adding meat drippings for flavoring if we had saved any. If we didn't have extra milk we'd make it with water. Often, on cold mornings, we would make toast by laying the bread slices on the hot surface of the stove, then heat up some home-bottled tomato juice and pour it over the toast. It tasted very good, but did not sustain us until noon. Lunch beans took care of that. The same 'recipe' was used with milk which made a delicious milk toast.

Part of the time we had a few scrawny chickens that provided eggs when the weather wasn't too cold—a luxury —and sometimes a chicken became Sunday dinner. Occasionally, there was a cow that could be sacrificed for beef. Invariably at the dinner table, one of the boys would ask "what cow is this?" You know, between the chickens and the cows, then later my pet goat, I was becoming a vegetarian. When the subject came up at the table, I always left my chair and went outside, too sickened to finish my food.

Another thing we always had was bottled fruit. My father traded with orchard owners for peaches, apricots, pears and apples. We picked our own and gathered what had fallen on the ground if it was usable. How well I remember the itchy peach fuzz on my sticky, sweaty neck and arms as I peeled the peaches. We bottled it by the tub-fulls in the summer. It tasted extremely good and refreshing in the drab winters.

We also dried a lot of the riper fruit on boards, and more up on the tin porch roof. Of course the flies got on it. *My goodness, we were tough with good immune systems!* Not always did the flies take over, as a kid was often assigned to shoo them off with a leafy twig.

Growing up I had never heard of an ice box. Mr. Kleinman, who owned the meat market, also sold big blocks of ice. I suppose there were people who had ice boxes. About once a year we bought a chunk of ice for twenty cents and made ice cream in a hand-cranked freezer.

We had a fabricated alternative to the ice box. Our food cooler was a hand-built wooden frame covered with screen wire—not the flimsy stuff of today, but strong enough to stop any vermin from chewing their way in. It stood about five feet tall and was about two and a half feet square. Four or five shelves held the milk and other food, and the system was efficient enough to keep butter from melting. On top was a large pan filled with water and the whole thing was draped with gunny sacks which soaked up water from the pan to drip down all four sides. It was a system of open-air screens. Woe unto us when a dust devil came suddenly screaming through the yard, whipping up the cloth and peppering everything full of dirt. No cool milk for supper that day. The slightest breeze was all it took to keep the water-drenched gunny sacks cool. There were always flies swarming around hoping to get in, but we made sure they were kept out. I believe the flies followed the pioneers from Salt Lake to Rockville, then on to Hurricane. Their job was to annoy and contaminate. The feet of this wooden cooling container were set in tin cans which were kept filled with water and became moats to prevent ants from crawling up the legs and in through the wire mesh. One of the kids was assigned the task of adding water to the pan on top and keeping the leg pans filled. This makeshift contraption was kept outside under a vine roof, for extra cooling effect.

There was a sorghum mill about a block down the lane from us. Each fall the sugar cane was harvested. The long stalks were cut off near the ground and brought to the mill next to the field. A workman fed the cane stalks into a hopper which ground them up, extracting the juice, and leaving nothing but fibrous pulp. The juice squirted down into big oblong iron or steel vats. The hopper was fastened to one end of a long pole. The other end of the pole was attached to a hook on a horse's harness. The forlorn horse walked around in a circle for hours compressing the stalks and squeezing out the juice.

Eventually the first vat was full. Then the workman built a fire under the vat to cook the cane juice. As it cooked down, the liquid evaporated, reducing the concoction to a thick sorghum molasses syrup. The man would strain the foam off the top as it formed, and stir with a long stick to prevent the syrup from sticking to the bottom.

From the cooking vat, it siphoned into other vats as a very thick syrup. When done, the molasses was ladled into gallon-sized tin buckets, and left to cool on a table, which was simply board planks laid across some barrels. Then lids were fastened securely. The whole process was a sweaty job, done in the late fall, but it was usually still hot weather. I remember the guy with this job wore dirty overalls and a sweat-stained shirt.

That molasses sure tasted good. We kids often went down there and got a cane stalk to twist and squeeze, sucking the sweet juice into our mouths. When twisted, the stalks had sharp edges and it was not unusual for us to cut our lips.

Mother sometimes made molasses candy. Often she would cook it to 'hard ball' stage and stretch it like taffy. She'd give each of us a gob to stretch. Being kids, we sometimes lost control and dropped some on the floor.

Another luxury we enjoyed came unexpectedly sometimes in midwinter when, on rare occasions snow blanket-ed the ground. We made use of it by filling our bowls with snow and covering it with cream, sugar, and a dash of vanilla extract. We relished that 'ice cream'. However, we were admonished not to eat the first snow of the season as it was unclean. According to common belief, the first snowfall cleaned any impurities from the air, and from then on it was good, clean snow. Other than the blue-gray fluff of smoke caused by the whole town firing up their stoves to warm up and cook breakfast on winter mornings; there was no pollution in Hurricane.

Dark Nights

One bleak winter day when I was five, I stood by my mother, one hand clutching her coat, and watched a man with a spike protruding from the inside of each black boot, descend from a pole near our property. He had shut off the power. There would be no electricity in our house for the next two years.

I was already afraid of the dark. And indeed, it was a dark day for our family, now confronting life through the hazy smoke of a dim kerosene lamp.

Mother's Molasses Candy

1 Cup Molasses

1 Cup Heavy Cream

1 Cup Sugar

Cook to medium-hard ball stage—check by dropping some candy into cold water.

She usually added a dash of baking soda before pouring out onto a buttered plate. Walnuts are a good addition, too.

For some reason, with the lights turned off, it seemed to be colder in our house. The north wind pushed forcefully through the cracks around doors and windows. There were always drafts to chill our spines and cause the lamp flame to flicker. It dipped and swayed almost being extinguished. We stuffed rags around the windows and poked old coats under the doors to shut out the gusting, icy wind.

Perhaps the most urgent incomplete part of the house was the bathroom. The fixtures were in but there was no water hook-up. Draftiness was miniscule compared to the horror of being forced to go outside. On those frigid days and nights, it was a matter of life and death to get psyched up enough to venture out to the "outhouse." Such a simple thing as answering the call of nature was way beyond reason. Life was not very pleasant right then. Winter just compounded the discomfort by freezing any exposed parts. Finding our way in the dark—no flashlights then—and finding the way back was just as hard, as there wasn't a window on that side of the house.

This was not unique with us. The whole town was subject to the outhouse blues.

Almost everyone had an outhouse but it still seemed an indignity to use one. Urgency helped, but one had to really be desperate to warrant dashing out into the cold.

One time when Aunt Philene was inside their outhouse, her son, Orlo, threw a rock at it. She emerged as if on a rocket exclaiming, "*I've heard of people getting the s*^#* scared out of them!*"

Clean Days

Wash day was almost too horrendous to talk about. This ordeal lasted all day, winter or summer, and, even though we didn't have very many clothes per person, it added up to a veritable mountain with nine kids and two adults. Add to that the kitchen towels and bath towels, although we shared the use of the bath towels. I don't recall having any bed sheets as we have these days. I believe we had some made from f*actory* material, a little coarser than the unbleached muslin of today. In winter it was flannel sheets. We did *not* wash the sheets every week.

Since it was such a chore, and the kids needed to help, we laundered on Saturdays. Wash days consisted of more than just doing the work. Sometimes we fought over who's turn it was to do what. Mother nagged us all day to keep us going and we kids nagged each other to show our discontent.

The setup was three, number three, tin tubs. The outside of one was black with soot as it perched on three strategically located rocks so a fire could be built under it. It was dreadful when white clothes accidentally touched the outside of that blackened tub. The other two tubs sat side by side on a wooden bench. All three were filled by the older boys carrying buckets of water from a tap across the yard. The black tub was fired up and a bar of homemade lye-and-lard soap was added, which gave the water a milky look. The second tub had clear water for rinsing and the third was doctored up with a dash of 'bluing'. This process consisted of taking small, chalky, intensely blue balls tied up in a thin rag, and swishing it around in the water. The water took on a bluish tinge that whitened the clothes and kept them from becoming dingy and yellowish, or 'tattle-tale gray' as the old ads claimed. Bluing required my mother's expertise, as a touch of blue brightened the white things just a little—unless you got too much and it tinged everything blue. Our soap was not great, but it was all we had.

The first batch, beginning with the whites, was put into the tub of boiling water. The agitator was a primitive contraption similar to a plumber's plunger. It was a metal thing shaped something like an upside down tin can with sections inside that caused a suction when plunged up and down in the tub of clothes. A wooden pole like a broom handle was screwed into the bottom end. Gripping this pole, we vigorously plunged up and down until we believed the clothes to be clean. We each took a 15-minute turn running the agitator punch, which took a toll on the arm muscles and shoulders. The stuck-on soil in areas like grimy collars and cuffs, were scrubbed by hand on the wash board. This was a wooden-framed, corrugated piece of metal about fourteen inches wide and about fifteen inches high with 'feet' that stood in the bottom of the tub. The top of the washboard leaned against the inside of the tub and dirty spots were forcefully rubbed up and down on the sudsy washboard. I remember a road in town named Washboard Road.

We'd lift the hot clothes out of the first wash tub with a broom handle, or other stick. Then try to wring them out —it wasn't easy wringing hot water out of the clothes so that they could be put in the first rinse water. The next batch was put in the hot tub as we moved to rinse the first batch. These were sloshed around until the soap was rinsed out. Each item was again wrung out with strong hands then dropped into the third, and final bluing tub. Incidentally this was the cleanest tin tub, with not much soap scum build-up. Therefore it doubled as our bathtub.

This wash, rinse, hand-wring process was done whether the cold north wind was blowing or not. The batches kept coming as we continued to wash. The job usually started early and ended late in the day. It was back- breaking work and all but the littlest kids helped. But it was my mother who got the brunt of the work.

A large tin pan was used to carry the 'washing' over to the fence about 50 feet away. The fence was net wire with one barbed wire strung above it to keep animals from trying to get over the fence. We had no clothes pins most of the time, we just draped the wet laundry over the wire. The barbs helped to keep the laundry in place, but barbs are not safe, as they would sometimes snag holes in the cloth.

Windy winter days were most miserable with our hands freezing along with the laundry. The clothes flattened into sheets of ice and stuck to the fence. We preferred not to leave colored, wet clothes on the line overnight because freezing faded them.

Starting in early spring, for a couple of months, wash days were not hampered by weather.

Then the months of summer struck and it meant that the scorching sun beating down on our heads was the other extreme. As we stood by the hot 'black' tub punching the steaming clothes we suffered with horrible sweltering heat, and we sweated and panted until fall. Often some of us had no shoes in the summer to protect our feet from the blisteringly hot ground. Those without shoes borrowed from someone else in the family not using their shoes at the moment. Even when the summer wind blew, it just helped to dry the clothes, its hot blast not really helping to alleviate our heat stroke.

Then gritting our teeth, we headed into winter wash days with courage. Not courage so much—we were just forced into doing what was necessary.

During all this heavy work, mother was obliged to fix three meals a day and clean up the meal residue, too. She required the older kids to help, but getting them to do the work was probably harder than doing it herself. Her discipline skills were lacking. She was a large woman, five-feet-eight tall and usually weighed around 160 pounds. The fact that she was pregnant every two years, didn't excuse her from the arduous work that was always there for her to do. Dad did not help her with anything around the house. He did expect us kids to help.

Today it's sheer pleasure to throw a batch of clothes into the washing machine and have them washed, dried and be done in slightly more than an hour. I also enjoy hanging them outside on the clothesline to let the sunny, Arizona breeze dry them in half an hour—even faster than the dryer, more invigorating, and cost effective, to boot. When your beginnings are humble enough, you can appreciate the most simple things.

Years later when my six children had the misfortune to live with me on a poverty level, their hardships were on a much higher scale than mine had been. Although they were deprived of many things, their bare necessities were met. They always had electricity, a bathroom, (albeit with no heat in our bathroom in Salt Lake), at least two bedrooms, and a washing machine. And to some extent, more food. When our washing machine stopped functioning, my two teen-aged boys made a down payment on a washer and dryer then worked after school and on Saturdays making payments until their loan was paid off. They worked at *Mrs. J. G. McDonald's Chocolate Factory* which was a couple of blocks from home. They did their own laundry. My oldest daughter also contributed to the family. With her after school job as a secretary, she bought us carpeting. Eventually, while he was still in high-school, my younger son bought the family a TV, a portable black-and-white. My children were always very resourceful like their ancestors before them.

Illustration 20: Alvin and Ann (Pickett) Hall Family. All eleven of us: clean and in clean clothes, no doubt.. (Photo: Courtesy Thelma Hall)

Clean as an Old Tin Tub

On Saturday nights the whole family bathed so we would be clean for church on Sunday. We'd fill water buckets at the kitchen sink, carry them across the large kitchen to our cast-iron cook-stove, and pour the water into kettles. When there was enough warm water to start a bath in a number three tin tub on the floor, the washing ceremony was begun by dunking the youngest kid in to get scrubbed. Then the next child up the chronological ladder was rotated through. With each succeeding child a pan of hot water was added to the rapidly cooling tub water. The bath water quickly turned to the color of the ground outside. We had no scales then, but I could guarantee that the kids weighed less and the tub water weighed more with each cleaned child. The little ones were put to bed after their turn in the water.

I don't believe I dared to think about it then, but now it haunts me wondering about there being nothing to stop those little kids from urinating in the community bath water. About halfway through us kids, the tub was carried outside, dumped, and a fresh tub was started—sheer luxury for the lucky one next in line.

Except in summer, being the only warm room in the house, we all had to stay in the kitchen during bath time. Not much privacy. For the older ones, we ringed the tin tub with tall-backed kitchen chairs and hung towels over them. While we waited for the little ones to finish their baths, we sat at the table and read by the lamplight or played cards: *Old Maid* or *Kersene*. Mother played a lot of solitaire so she managed to keep us in a deck of cards, although they were usually badly bent with lopped off corners.

My parents finished up bath day when everyone else was in bed. With all the Saturday washing, our skin was like prunes by bedtime.

Only about once a month, on Saturday mornings, we'd wash our hair. For shampooing, we used a pan. Then, if you had dark hair, you added a spoonful of vinegar in the pan of rinse water. For light-headed kids, you added a couple of squirts of lemon juice in the pan of rinse water. This served to cut the soap scum from the hair. Then we combed out our wet hair and parted it in the middle.

Regardless of the weather, with cold breezes drifting through the kitchen in winter, we never missed a Saturday bath. We were required to have a bath once a week whether we needed it or not.

Simple Pleasures

With all the hard work my mother had to do, she still found time for little pleasures in life. On the rocky lava soil she grew a few flowers. At the front, which faced south, hollyhocks and orange corn lilies flourished. Along the east side she had made a terrace with black rocks. Myrtle vines did very well there. Their small deep purple flowers looked very pretty. That was the extent of our growing except for the volunteer stuff, such as milkweed and Russian thistle, which grew profusely. Ouch, when the thistles dried—it was usually necessary to go bare-footed, partly to save your shoes for town, and partly because your shoes were worn out and or you had none.

School Days

Our school house was a flat-topped, one story structure. The bell on top was about a foot tall and did its job well. The loud gonging of the bell was crucial in calling people together, whether for a community event or an emergency. But its main function was to call us to school. Its ring was so loud it could be heard throughout the town and reached our ears a mile away.

The school custodian, Mr. Tweedie, was a thin, tall man with black hair and a pale face who wore farmer's overalls. I found out later that his paleness was because of illness and he did not live a long life, leaving his family of five children.

On school days Mr. Tweedie rang the bell long and loud at 8:00 am. Then at 8:30 just a few short rings. And by 9 o'clock, when he gave it a couple of dings, students were supposed to be in their seats with their hands folded on their wooden desks.

Illustration 21: It's me, Glenna Hall, about 1933. (From class photo by R.D. Adams)

I always came in gasping for air, barely on time, having run most of the way. Not surprisingly, I always won the foot races on the Fourth of July for my age group.

On winter days, starting out for school before the sun was up took courage. But I had no choice. I was so cold I shivered, then just ran to keep warm. When I got to school I sat on my frozen, stiff hands until they thawed enough to hold my pencil.

In those days, there wasn't a school lunch program so we all had to go home to eat. We called the noon meal "dinner". Back then, farmers ate their largest meal at noon. Ravenous, we hurried home to gulp down potato and onion soup, or pinto beans with whole wheat bread. Then we fast-walked or ran back to school. I always got a 'side ache' from running after a meal. We were allotted an hour for dinner—going the mile home, eating, and returning. Making it back to school on time took skill and considerable dedication.

At four o'clock, there were always several kids in the pack as we made this trek for the fourth and last time of the

Illustration 22: School photos were taken by a local man named R.D. Adams. He used a tripod with a square, wooden camera perched on top, with a black cloth draped over it to keep out the light. He'd duck his head under the cloth, focus, and squeeze a bulb to take the picture. That's me, Glenna Hall, back row 5th from right. Mr. Gates', 5th grade class .—See Appendix A for names

day. Conditions were no better than they had been in the morning—sometimes worse, depending on the weather.

Heading west the sun was low in the sky as we trudged along the rutted road, which was sprinkled with fine black cinders.

On the worst days an icy north wind whipped up fine cinders stinging my legs even through my heavy long brown cotton stockings. Bitter cold froze us all. Biting wind froze our faces and ears, forcing us to scurry toward the shelter of home. Overhead, brittle power lines wailed an anthem as they sliced the wind. On days like this, my arms ached from carrying books and gripping my number two, yellow pencil in my frozen fist. Several kids trekked out our road and dropped off at their houses. Our house was the last one on the dirt road.

It was not always this cold. But I've never forgotten it. In late spring and early fall the *heat* was unbearable on that same trail going and coming from school.

On those cold days. when at last we were home from school, we all hovered around the big, black, cast iron kitchen stove to thaw out. If no bread was baking, we were allowed to open the oven door, put a stick of firewood in, and put our legs across it, poking our feet into the oven. How far we put them in depended on how hot the fire was. Sometimes we smelled burning rubber or leather. This invariably produced shrieking as the hot shoe burned the foot while the afflicted person scrambled to get it off. The shoe smoldered until it cooled off. Getting warm didn't come cheaply, nor without a lot of effort. Damaging a shoe was a sin. "Holy Moses, Heck Dogie!" was my father's epithet. Being a religious man, that was all the swearing he could muster.

One or another of us nearly always had a hole in the bottom of one or both of our shoes. We'd put cardboard in the shoe to cover the holes until father could "half sole" the shoes. With our large family, he was kept busy resoling them. He used an iron *last*, common in those days, which stood upside down on an iron platform. The upper part was shaped like the bottom of a shoe so that when the shoe was fitted onto this, the iron deflected the tacks when the sole was tacked on around the outside edges.

Theoretically, when hammered, the tacks bent over when coming in contact with the last. It was not a perfect solution because often a stray tack would later puncture the foot. By the time you got home to take the shoe off, this malfunction could cause a sizable hole in the foot. Putting cardboard in the shoe helped a little until dad could pull the tack out.

By the time we warmed up it was dark and our big family gathered around the long wooden, oil-cloth-covered kitchen table to eat our evening supper. What a sight—all ten of us (the last kid wasn't born yet), counting kids and parents, crowding around the big table with the oil lamp casting an eerie glow on our faces.

Our supper fare was always the same, bread and milk. We each crumbled bread into our tin bowls and filled it on up with milk from a 2-quart bottle. We preferred milk from the previous milking, not fresh and warm that had just been milked. Additions to our bread and milk, were green onions in the spring, and in winter it was honey which had hardened in the cold weather. Or we'd toast bread on the stove then top with butter and molasses. Great taste for grateful people. Everything that was food tasted good in those days. Although simple fare, there must have been enough nutrition in the food we ate. Except for three siblings who died much too early, and of various causes, we haven't lost any siblings in forty-eight years.

When there was enough cream on top of the milk, it was skimmed off and churned into butter by whipping it by hand with a spoon until it turned into butter. Or, cottage cheese was made from surplus milk. The milk was soured, then the whey was separated out. What was left was cottage cheese. On rare occasions there was enough for my mother to make cheese, pressing it into a small wooden box. Our cows grazed on weeds and sage brush on the almost barren hillside. Not much grass grew there. Sometimes there was the flavor of sagebrush in the milk. Or worse—chaparral! Chaparral is a lovely refreshing fragrance after a rain, but a bitter taste in milk.

Later, after we moved to the four room house, there were times when we had a surplus of milk. The cow feed was better and produced good tasting milk. My mother sold three quarts a day to the Isoms. Blanche Isom's boy, Jack, always came to get it. It was five cents a quart. One day Blanche came to our house quite upset and accused mother of selling her “skimmed” milk. My mother knew that wasn't so. They questioned Jack, then his sister, Sidney. It turned out that Sidney had been drinking the cream off the glass jug then filling it up with water. Poor kid was hungry.

The cows were rotated so that when some were 'fresh' from having a calf, they could give milk, and the others were in-between calving.

Mother kept us in bread by baking several loaves every three or four days. She occasionally made raisin bread and cinnamon buns. Yum. I'm sure “bread” had a deeper meaning in the Bible—bread is the staff of life. Our bread was made with unrefined, unbleached flour. For a more healthy loaf, ground whole wheat was added. It was, indeed, the staff of our lives. It supported and sustained us.

Before the days of store-bought yeast, a potato “start” was required to get the bread to rise. Otherwise it would have been like a rock. A couple of potatoes were cooked in water, then allowed to age or ferment. Some of the “starter” was used in the bread and the rest was saved for the next batch. Water was added to keep it going.

Sometimes a housewife would neglect her “start” and it would dry up. A “start” could always be borrowed from a neighbor. The texture of the bread was coarse and surrounded by a thick hard crust, and when sliced, produced a lot of crumbs. At supper, with all of us crumbling our bread getting ready to eat, crumbs were flying across the table and onto the floor.

After supper each night we took turns clearing the

table. After taking the dishes over to be washed at the sink, the next step was what we called "scrape" the table. You used a knife to scrape off the crumbs into a pan held just under the edge of the table. These were saved for the chickens or given to the cat. We always had a cat or two around to keep the mice in check. It was almost an artistic ritual as you scraped the crumbs from side to side getting them funneled just right and directing them to the point of pushing them over the edge into the pan. Then the oil-cloth-covered table was wiped off with a damp dish rag.

As soon as the table was clean, we gathered around it to do our homework, our pale ghostly faces bent over our books and papers in the dim glow of the kerosene lamp, the dark of the kitchen surrounding us. Think of being spot-lighted with a dim light, since the glow reached only a few feet from the lamp. There was surely stress with homework when we had to crowd each other just to get a share of the light. As you can imagine we never had to worry about glare on our books and papers.

An old cliché my mother used to say was meant to promote good health:

After breakfast, work awhile.

After dinner, rest awhile.

After supper, walk a mile.

We never did. With all the running back and forth to school, we just did our homework in the dim night, and went to bed.

Fun and Games

When I was a child actual toys were rare. We played in the dirt devising ways to entertain ourselves. From the sagebrush and lava-rock-strewn hills adjoining our land at the outside edge of town, we searched for and found little dried animal bones, probably the remains of rabbits. We used them as farm animals. Using small rocks, we defined our landscape. We sectioned off little corrals. Our herds were kept in these: horses in one, cows in another. We created pigs and chickens, as well.

There was no gender distinction. Boys and girls all played in the dirt, using our imaginations to create replicas of the adult world. Improvising, each kid set up his own domain and acted out his own agenda.

Another specialized skill we had was carving model cars. We used scraps of wood left over from the house building. The cars we knew about were Model T and Model A Fords and Studebaker's, as well as generic coupes and sedans. My brother, Gerald, even scooped out a rumble seat, which was a nice touch.

- We played Kick-The-Can. Sometimes a kid would kick a can all the way home from town.
- We made stilts using a hammer and nail to poke holes in the bottom end of two cans, then looped heavy strings through the holes. We'd hold onto the string loops and walk on the cans, lifting them along by the strings.
- We made a more industrious kind of stilts by fitting a block of wood near the top of a couple of two-by-fours. That block was for your foot to stand on. Then a leather strap was looped from the block to the top of the two-by-four to secure the foot. The length/height

of the stilts (2x4's) depended on how brave a kid was. They ranged from a foot high to two or three feet tall.

- Flat iron loops ten to twelve inches diameter were sometimes available. A narrow board about two feet long was fitted on one end with a tin can lid. It was bent up on each side to form a groove that the hoop fit into. A kid would run along keeping the hoop rolling. There were no couch potatoes in that day. And no fat kids.
- The boys carved pistols from wood. A clothes pin was secured to the butt end. The ammo was made from narrow loops of rubber from an old bicycle inner tube. One end was looped on the pointy end of the gun, the other end was stretched into the clothes pin. To shoot, you just squeezed the clothes pin. The tight rubber band went off and hit somebody. Hopefully not in the eye.
- We liked to make up plays and perform them for whoever we could get to watch.
- Our hopscotch format was marked off in the dirt with a stick. The taws (markers) were small pieces of old colored glass worn smooth from weathering in the sand and grit. Across the road was a vacant area where we could get broken glass that had been dumped. Each kid picked a different color for his taw. Or sometimes a choice rock was used.

The summer afternoons in the heat were seemingly endless. Mostly we played in the shade of the house. Also, we went down the lane near the sorghum mill and played in the irrigation ditch. The water was muddy and only about a foot deep, but it felt good to lay on our stomachs and wallow in it. We called it *mud crawl*.

While at the ditch, we scraped clay from the banks

and formed little dishes, setting them in the sun to bake dry. They made great props for our play house scenarios.

Coming back home, if we were wearing any shoes, we'd have to scrape the mud off before entering the house. Most houses had part of a broken shovel embedded into the cement of the porch. Or the foot scraper was bolted to the boards of the porch, whatever the case may be.

To this day, 75 years later, in my mind I can re-create the musty smell of that slimy, muddy ditch lined with willows and weeds.

Another highlight of our summertime experiences was monitoring caterpillar larvae to see them becoming Monarch butterflies. There were milkweed plants on our land out west of the house. Cows were kept out of that area as milkweed was called "loco weed" and if the cows ate it they would act "loco" — goofy. It began with finding a black and light green striped worm clinging on a milkweed stem. We would pick the stem and bring it to the house where we'd nail it to a wall. In about two weeks the worm turned itself inside out which formed a chrysalis, an oval shaped, pale green, cocoon, with a prong on one end which was stuck to the stem. It was about the size of a short little finger. A few days later the cocoon began to open and a beautiful Monarch butterfly worked its way out. It perched there, clinging to the stem for an hour or so, and flapped its new wings experimentally until it was able to fly away.

We made corn silk dolls. We collected the little beginnings of corn growing out of the side of large corn ears. We used these miniature corn ears as dolls. We imagined the corn silk as flowing robes.

We Depression kids were not as sophisticated as today's children but we were very creative and valued and appreciated what we had.

Remedies

In those days, childhood ailments consisted of colds, flu and the usual communicable diseases such as mumps, measles, whooping cough, and scarlet fever. For one of these, a red flag was hung on your gate to indicate you were quarantined. No one was allowed in or out of the yard.

Our medicine was mustard plasters, castor oil and Brigham tea. Brigham Young had recommended steeping twigs from a certain spiny shrub found on the hillsides outside of town. It was purported to be a blood cleanser. Therefore, my dad concocted this spring tonic by boiling it until it was so strong and awful-tasting that we had to be forced to drink it. If you steep a milder version, it isn't so bitter, it's still very astringent and tastes a little like pine.

Old-time remedies are often the best. For ant or wasp stings, we'd put a pinch of baking soda on the sting then spoon a little vinegar on it to form a foamy frizz. It takes away the pain.

Then others, are just plain zany: to get rid of a wart, you'd "charm it off" by rubbing a dirty rag on it then burying the rag. Sooner or later the wart would drop off. Or, my uncle would stand there rubbing the wart while distracting the person with conversation, and, you know, sooner or later that wart would drop off.

Another thing I remember from childhood is that there were sometimes five cuttings of alfalfa in the summer. The smell of new-mown hay created a powerful, heady aroma that's hard to describe. You could say it had a fresh, green "flavor" to it as you snuffed it up your nose. Pure chlorophyll.

Nearby cow corrals had an overwhelmingly distinctive odor that counter-balanced the glorious alfalfa essence.

Incidentally, sometimes cows or other animals got loose and went through town foraging on whatever they could find, vegetable gardens, flowers, or lawns. There was a hired employee in charge of rounding them up and putting them in the stray pen. It would cost the owners ten cents a head to get them out. Thus, we had animal control services even back then.

Pranks

Depression, or not, there had to be outlets for amusement. The young men of the town provided ample diversion, much to the annoyance of the adults. Life in a small town before radio and television may not have been much different even without The Depression; especially for the mischievous older boys. They created their own fun at the expense of others, by playing outrageous pranks on their fellow townspeople. They stole watermelons. They stole chickens to fry over a campfire—a regular event. They were able to 'hit' the coops and be away before the squawking chickens aroused their owners. Or, it might have been that someone was lying in wait for them and the thieves would hastily retreat through a rain of buckshot. The sound was deafening.

One time four of the culprits were apprehended and turned over to the sheriff—who was nothing more than a deputized farmer. The chicken thieves were jailed in a room at the back end of an old abandoned adobe building which had previously been the bank. Each day someone brought them food, probably more than bread and water. The jailbirds seemed strangely indifferent to being locked up and didn't eat much of the food. Their providers wondered why they were not grateful for the food. People were still losing chickens and it was later discovered why, when one of the prisoners bragged to a friend who came to visit him at the window. He made the mistake of bragging in the presence of his friend's little brother. The secret was out. They had possession of a skeleton key which they kept under a loose adobe brick in their cell. Letting themselves out each night, they would raid a chicken coop, then go out to the fields south of town to cook it and continue their feasting. They'd be back at the jail with plenty of time to get a good night's sleep on a full stomach.

The extracurricular activities of the boys were more or less seasonal. A prevalent Halloween prank was tipping over out-houses all over town. So many boys were involved that it amounted to a team sport. One such incident brought a scream from a man who was inside when his outhouse went over. I was told it was a prominent businessman, Harvey Dalton. The meanest part would be to tip it over with the door on the ground trapping the person inside. This was the plight of Harvey Dalton.

It was the custom to create paper valentine's for your favorite person. It went like this: after dark on Valentine's Day, you deposited the valentine on the door step, banged on the door, and dashed around the house so as not to be caught. Sometimes, the guys would tie a string to the card, hide behind a nearby bush, and jerk it away just as the recipient reached down to pick it up.

This prank was working well for my cousin, Willis, then the door was answered by the girl's father. Her dad answered the door the next time, too, stamping at the card and still couldn't catch it. He got so riled up at not being fast enough that his determination reached a fever pitch. He stood behind the door waiting for the trickster. He needed to know who was pulling his chain, so to speak. Willis returned with a fool-proof plan and several guys as witnesses. As soon as he hit the door and ran, sure enough, the father stomped his foot fast and hard down on the porch, only to realize it had landed in a pan of fresh, runny, cow manure.

In summer almost everyone slept outside as the houses were too hot and suffocating. They moved their beds or cots out under the trees or simply slept on the lawn with a mattress, or just blankets underneath and a sheet on top. The clever ones located their beds on the shady, west side of the house to avoid the morning sun.

At the top of the list for summer sport? Ducking. Boys would sneak around in the night and drench sleepers with buckets full of water, then sprint away to avoid getting caught. Often a 'ducked' person leaped out of bed and gave chase in his underwear.

One particular night a group of boys, one of which was my brother, placed the end of a hose in the Sandberg's summer bed. The boys waited for them to retire and settle down to sleep. Then someone carefully turned on the tap a little at a time, drizzling the water in slowly. After a few minutes they heard Mrs. Sandberg exclaim, "*why* *Chauncy!* *What* *are* *you doing?*"

Some kids even thought it amusing to ring cowbells at night. This was not too successful though, as they were easy to track.

I had an uncle who was a mean character as a young man. In fact, all his life he was pretty ornery. He simply got a lot of glee out of tormenting people. One incident happened at peach picking time at the orchard. Planks were set up for the packers to arrange peaches in boxes. Uncle Lafe sauntered along behind the packers, usually girls, and twitched them on the neck with a leafy twig. Thinking they were being bugged by flies, they'd swat at their necks repeatedly. This was very distracting and slowed down the assembly line process, not to mention the fact that they got the itchy peach fuzz on their necks. They eventually discovered it was Lafe aggravating them. Even so, he did not stop. Mrs. Hastings finally erupted with "*oh, I'm so mad I could swear. Gosh, gosh, gosh!*"

There was a character in town, who as a child, was subjected to a different kind of learning experience—bullying. He did survive it and turned out to be an outstanding citizen, helping people out whenever he saw the opportunity.

He was the oldest of the boys in the family, causing his mother to dote on him as a young child. Her pet name for him was "Sonny Doll". Can you imagine what happened to him once the children in town got hold of this special nick-name? A mother's love caused horrible consequences for her child. He was not a member of any group. He didn't fit in anywhere. I'm not sure how much public school he attended.

My earliest memory was of him riding his bicycle with a shovel over his shoulder on his way out to the edge of town to his farm job. Invariably, from off in the distance the call "*Oh, Sunny Doll-l-l-l*", rang out and he dropped the bike and fiercely ran off toward the kids who called him that name. He chased with raised shovel ready to do damage, but the kids had scattered and he couldn't catch any of them.

Another time my teen-aged brother, Gerald, and some other boys called out the dreaded name. He took off after them as they escaped through a fence. Catching up to my brother who had stopped at the fence, he asked menacingly, "did you call me that name?" My brother looked him in the eye and said coolly, "would I be standing here if I had called you that?" The young man walked away and my brother proceeded to unhook his coat from the barbed wire fence which had caught him as he was trying to get away.

This torture and harassment was generational.

Children grew up and passed this dastardly curse down to their kids. They may not have purposely passed it on, but they all heard about it by word-of-mouth and it never ended for this poor guy. The family house on Main Street has been torn down and replaced with a park-like area. Amazingly, the big mulberry tree that stood in front of the house is still there—it's huge! I remember seeing his mother sweeping the dirt from her doorway and the yard under that tree.

Another nick-name was "Creepy ____". Who knows how he got the name? One report says that he had lost a hand, due to an accident, and had a prosthetic. Metal pincers. Even though he endured this nick-name, he too, was an exemplary citizen.

People, especially children, can be quite mean spirited, and I am wondering why I would pass on information like this even now. At some point, the stories should probably just fade away. I am using these examples to show that there are many types of surviving. Everyone has personal stories of childhood. Some good. Some bad. We try to only remember the Good Old Days with nostalgia.

Other names I remember: Rulon Isom, nicknamed *Spud* or *Tater* was the town butcher; *Topsy Berry Bangs* had long, straggly hair; the *Stratton drop-off* was a haircut that looked like a bowl had been fitted over the top of a boy's head and shaved up his neck to the edge of the bowl. Some things you just don't forget.

Celebrations

The local celebrations—4th of July, 24th of July, and Peach Days—were much more important than it would seem, for their designated purpose of respect. These events were some of the few times the whole town mingled socially. Everyone who lived on the north side of State Street belonged to the north ward. Those on the other side of the street were south-warders. Going to church in our own wards, we barely crossed paths with each together. School was the exception, but the adults relied on these valuable social functions to keep in touch.

Easter

We started preparing weeks in advance for Easter by decorating shoe boxes with crepe paper. We were glad to get them as these were our Easter baskets. Crepe paper of various colors cost ten cents a package. The glue to paste the crepe paper on was made by simmering flour and water to a sticky mess. Baling wire wrapped with several layers of crepe paper became the basket handle. Hard boiled eggs were dyed by soaking them in hot crepe paper water. An egg was put in a nest of green confetti. A half deviled ham sandwich completed the picnic lunch. One year, my mother somehow had gotten hold of fifteen cents with which she bought a few colored candy eggs in various sizes. There were also little fluffy yellow chicks with orange wire legs. We were then ready to set off on our Easter walk with church or school class. Both participated in the Easter walk.

Compare this with the kids of today, rich by most world standards. They are driven to the supermarket and made to choose from hundreds of baskets to find the right one suitable for an Easter Bunny. Include a fluffy toy and chocolate Easter eggs, and you have a tradition of sorts.

Fourth of July

On the Fourth of July, Independence Day, the townspeople went all out. Either they appreciated their forefathers winning their freedom from England in 1776, or they were simply ready to get some excitement in their lives by congregating downtown on the town square to celebrate.

At daybreak a cannon blast went off which was heard throughout the valley. The World War I Legionnaires always handled firing the cannon. Shorty Bradshaw was the self-appointed leader and took over the cannon shot every year. I don't know how the cannon got to Hurricane.

Then as the sun came up—it would have been about 5:30—a two-ton, flatbed truck with side racks lumbered down Main Street. It was filled with people sitting on benches singing patriotic songs. My mother was always there. There was even a piano up against the cab of the truck on which Jesse Jepson pounded out chords for the songs. Mother's good friend, Annie Covington, and another harmonica player could also be heard. The truck drove slowly through all the streets in town. The music was rousing and expertly sung.

A lull then settled over the town while everyone milked their cows, got breakfast over with, combed their hair and dressed their kids. Excitement was in the air as the townspeople anticipated a day off from their sweaty and hot farming chores or housework.

The parade was scheduled to begin at ten o'clock, but people were gathering under the elm and cottonwood trees downtown on the square long before ten. Men and boys all wore Levi Strauss pants or bib overalls and blue chambray shirts, often with patched elbows. Women and girls wore homemade cotton "house dresses" in various prints and polka dots.

A patriotic theme was depicted on decorated cars and frisky horses with their manes and tails braided, and streamers attached to their bridle reins. Some of the riders wore fancy beaded leather gloves. Most wore neckerchiefs and cowboy hats. I don't know where the parade committee got little flags on sticks, but they were plentiful and posted in various places.

After the parade the crowd dispersed and walked home to eat their noon meal. Re-converging in mid-afternoon they were ready to start the races and other contests.

The foot races were started with the six-year-olds. They had their toes on a line drawn in the dirt. The race master yelled *"GO!"* and they ran lickety-split to the finish line. Next the seven-year-olds, and on up the ranks. I always won in my age group. The reason, of course, was that I ran so much to and from school. A mile is a pretty good run.

Several people participated in the three-legged-race. A gunny sack was shared by two people, each with one leg in the sack. They all stood at the starting line. "GO!" was called and they raced to the finish line. Coordinating was very important. They often wound up flat on the ground if they couldn't get a rhythm going. This race had categories for kids, teens, and even adults. It was always fun to try it and fun to watch.

While I got the winner's nickel, everyone involved got an ice cream cone from a hand-cranked freezer. Aunt Bertha Hall made the ice cream and dipped up the cones for us. To this day, I remember how delicious those ice cream cones tasted! Especially after the exertion of running in the hot afternoon.

Lemonade stands, candy and popcorn stands were set up. These things must have been cheap, a nickel or a penny maybe, because most people didn't have cash on hand to buy much. A nickel or a penny would buy *something!* In later years hot dog stands came on the scene.

The day wore on into evening for the open air dance. The "dance hall" was simply a large cement slab. There was always a dance. And sometimes, not always, there was a fireworks display, after which everyone went home tired and happy.

24th of July

The 24th of July was also celebrated in Hurricane, but perhaps with a little less hoopla. The hardy Mormon pioneers first reached the Salt Lake Valley on July 24th, 1847 and Brigham Young proclaimed, "this is the place".

The parade commemorating this event depicted a reenactment of the pioneers trudging across the mid-western plains pulling hand carts heavy with babies, young children, and belongings. Also in the parade were horse-drawn wagons carrying people dressed in pioneer garb—women and children in long-sleeved, dresses with long skirts and wearing home made cloth sun bonnets.

If you've never seen a pioneer sun bonnet, picture this: the back covering the crown area is gathered and pouf-y. There is a very wide brim, sometimes four inches, but more likely six to eight inches, and there are long, wide ties which make a nice big bow under the chin. Or if the bow is tied close to the ends of the streamers, you can hang the bonnet down your back when not wanting to wear it.

Illustration 23: Sun Bonnet with neck protection.

Illustration 24: Sun Bonnet with tie straps.

The rest of the procedure for the Twenty-fourth of July was similar to the Fourth with races and games. The whole town enthusiastically turned out. They loved any excuse to congregate that went beyond church meetings on Sundays, and Pioneer Day was another welcome break from the mundane and daily chores.

Peach Days

As time went on, both in town and out in the fields, orchards matured and produced a wide variety of fruit trees bearing prize-winning fruit. There were peaches, apricots, plums, apples, cherries and nut trees abounding with walnuts, pecans and almonds. The townspeople also grew grapes—purple, red, and white. As well as orchards, there were numerous kinds of melons, and a full range of vegetables.

Illustration 25: Peach Day August 15, 1911. (Photo: Courtesy Victor Hall)

Hurricane was becoming well known for its peaches, at least in Utah. Therefore, another celebration was called for. The town leaders decided on a two-day fair to be held in late August at the peak of the fruit season. The fair was called *Peach Days*. The high school auditorium was set up

Illustration 26: Peach Day Fruit Display. (Photo: Courtesy Victor Hall)

with platforms ten feet deep along the east end, which slanted back to the wall for best viewing of the exhibits. Entrance doors were at each end of this display.

The containers holding the produce were low-sided wooden crates. They were artistically arranged in a colorful array that was a joy to look at: red/gold Elberta peaches, white cling peaches, purple plums and prunes, green gage plums, orange apricots, green and yellow pears, and purple, red, and green grapes. Also black figs, and red pomegranates. These were all separated with narrow rows of pecans, walnuts and almonds.

At one end, a section contained a variety of melons: green watermelons, white watermelons, honeydew, casabas and cantaloupes. The other end displayed vegetables: corn, tomatoes, carrots, green beans, potatoes, and various kinds of colorful squash.

Angled across a few feet of space to the south side was a table laden with quart bottles of home processed food—'canning' was a skill in itself. Peach halves were arranged in bottles, round side up. There were bottles filled with whole apricots and whole plums, purple and green. I even remember seeing colored grapes preserved in bottles. There were also strawberry, and other kinds of, jams and jellies. Next to these were pickles, green relishes, and red chili sauces.

Along the north wall of the auditorium stood tables holding elaborate hand made crafts. There were crocheted doilies and bed spreads, tatted lace table clothes, And many well-made original design dresses and shirts.

On the west end, mounted on the wall, hung elaborate, intricately designed block quilts. Some with hundreds of harmoniously colored pieces. I liked to admire the hand-sewing on the quilts, and I guess I took an interest in sewing at a young age. In my seventh grade home economics class, I won the apron-making contest. I received a fancy little lapel pin. My bib-style apron was made of pink cotton cloth with blue bias tape neatly applied around all the edges.

The day before the fair opened, a committee studied the exhibits and selected first, second, and third places and put the winning ribbons on each item.

To round off the celebration, there were sometimes horse races at the north end of town where they had set up a rodeo ground. The men took some kind of joy in knowing how to make horses buck and showing off their skills. Many knew how to throw a lasso and drop a dogie (a weaned calf) to the ground and tie three legs together.

The American Legion sponsored boxing matches and an open-air dance in the evening on the second day. Local musicians made up the band. I remember Donna

Sandberg bouncing on the bench as she played the piano. Strange what a kid notices.

When Peach Days ended on the second night, watermelons were sliced and served to everyone. A few Indians who had come to town for the festivities sat along the edge of the street waiting for the melon feast. I remember an Indian lady giving birth to a baby on the ground behind the schoolhouse.

One time, my sister, Lorna, was in line for something and an Indian lady swatted her on the shoulder admonishing her to, "hutty up".

Election Days

As to town politics, campaign songs at election time were sung by a group of people riding around in the back of a big truck.

One of the songs I remember was sung to the tune of a Mormon Hymn, *In Our Lovely Deseret:* "David Hirschi, he's not slim, but he's full of pluck and vim..." He was running for Mayor on the Republican ticket, and my mother was in the back of the truck singing as loud as she could manage.

On election days, a guy drove slowly around town shouting through a megaphone urging everyone to go downtown and vote. Some people didn't divulge who they would vote for. My grandma Pickett kept it a secret, giving not a hint of who she was voting for, even when we asked her directly. As I look back, I think she may have been a Democrat.

Christmas

Christmas was a given. Regardless of anyone's disadvantaged circumstances, they never neglected Christmas. We didn't get much but we always got *something*. Granted, many children were disappointed in the Santa Claus they had been taught to believe in, and the more kids in the family, the less each one got.

One of my memorable gifts was a dress my mother made for me. It was pink cotton splattered with small blue flowers. Blue bias tape finished off all the edges—neck, sleeves, hem. I am wearing it in the family photo. (p.53)

The most precious gift I ever received was a little electric lamp. I was eleven or twelve. My older brother made the wooden base in shop class. My mother bought the shade in St. George—blue silk with pink flowers and a dark blue fringe. A pull chain turned it on and off. The whole lamp was about fourteen inches tall. My mother had a small mirror which sat on top of the organ. She would put my lamp up there when she looked in that little mirror to get ready to go somewhere.

I also got a book called *Christmas in California*.

Simple gifts, given spontaneously, can create cherished memories, as well. When we were kids my Aunt Annabell sometimes gave my cousin, Stella, and me a chicken egg to trade to Graff's Mercantile. The egg was worth a penny, and for that, we each got a flat lollipop. I usually chose a transparent yellow one. The big round ones were called 'all-day suckers.' They also cost a penny. I always appreciated Aunt Annabelle being such a nice lady for gifting us with the eggs. She was a shy person who came to visit my mother once in awhile. She was not much of a gabber. She only stayed a few minutes—not like some of the others who stayed all afternoon.

My mind recalls other kids treasured gifts, too. Summers were extremely hot and there was no place to escape the heat. I remember when a boy of about twelve had received a new plaid wool coat from his grandmother who lived in Salt Lake City. It was a sweltering hot day in mid-August when he got it. There was a program being held in the school auditorium and it was intensely hot in the building. The only cooling was generated by many people waving fans or scraps of cardboard in front of their faces, and yet this boy was so thrilled to have a decent coat that he wore it all day even in that oven of an auditorium. I give that kid credit, he never passed out.

Depression as a Lifestyle

Growing up knowing nothing but the pall of poverty, seems to have set the pattern for my life. I didn't know how to be anything but poor. My dad used to say, "poor people have poor ways." I'm wondering if he thought there was something honorable about that.

During those years we were so conditioned to doing without that the Depression was not that much of a shift. It is sad to reflect that living with The Depression during my formative years made it so that I would not have hope for a better future. The biggest lesson learned from my family circumstances was my attitude of not striving for a better life. I just went with the flow, not expecting much and not getting much.

My parents, with harsh personalities, their struggles utterly daunting, were unable to instill a sense of security in their children. The Depression inflicted more than just a lack of money. It caused an emotional drain that went beyond the shortages. Worried as they must have been in their attempt to feed their family, my parent's concern for us did not translate into love. In fact, it could have amplified their lack of knowledge in rearing children. They raised us without any rhyme or reason. Neither of them had enough self-esteem to treat their children with respect or kindness. Life just happened to them. They quarreled a lot, with my mother, the more sensitive, making sure she appeared the victim. Her upbringing had taught her that women were not equal to men, and my dad believed in the religious principle of male hierarchy.

My mother's mother, Grandma Pickett, was an overly strict Englishwoman. She taught my mother to keep out of sight except to do house work. As a child mother was kept out of the kitchen so knew very little about preparing food and running a household.

Mother once told me about an event from her teen-age years: she was sixteen and had been invited to a summer afternoon birthday party. She was allowed to go but told to be home by six o'clock. The party host parents were making ice cream in the hand-crank freezer. It was not quite done at six o'clock. My mother anxiously watched the clock and explained to her friend's mother that she was supposed to leave. The lady said, "it will only be a few minutes more and I will talk to your mother about it." At ten minutes after six, her unsmiling mother appeared at the gate—just stood there glaring. Then she called to my mother, "Ann, you were supposed to be home at six." Her friend's mother asked if she could stay just a little longer so she could have ice cream with her friends. Absolutely not! She gave not an inch. Ann had to leave the party with several hours of daylight left. This would have been 1913 as she was born in 1897. She never really learned how to stand up for herself.

My parents did not know how to communicate with each other nor with their children, whom they scolded without reason. I suppose it came from their own insecurity. There was a lack of reassuring us that we were safe. Nor did they teach us to strive; that we were capable of accomplishment or reaching out to succeed. The subject never came up. They left everything up to church and school. They merely brought us into the world. Contrast that with today's children who reign over all.

Our births were not specifically planned. It was more like "ready or not, here we come". The Mormon doctrine to "multiply and replenish the earth" could have meant anything. My parents bought the story of lots of children.

Obviously their lives had not prepared them for

parenthood. Then The Depression put such a dark cloud over them that they were unable to function well without showing their stress and worries. I mention it only because the effects of their dysfunction on me were so destructive that my life has been very difficult. It has taken me a long time to become more or less emotionally healthy.

The one thing they were consistent in was requiring us to go to church. Who would teach their kids for them if we didn't go to church? We did have a choice of sorts—anyone who didn't go washed all the noon dishes. Sunday dinner always entailed a bunch of greasy pots and pans. Home-made bar soap was almost useless on greasy stuff. It left a definite scum on the dishes. A friend once asked me, “do you shine your glasses?” This meant rubbing them with a dry dish towel, similar to washing windows. We did not have glass tumblers—ours were good tin cups which lasted longer. It did take effort to rub the sludge off the dishes. They could not be left to drain dry. Then the dish towels had to be scrubbed on the washboard.

There were a few times when I chose to stay home from church and clean that mountain of dishes. That was the only time I was ever alone. I was always ill-at-ease around people. Any people. Even my immediate family. So washing the dishes was the only way I could get away from them.

Incidentally, our Sunday-go-to-meeting clothes were no different than our everyday clothes.

Federal Depression

Well into The Great Depression, President Roosevelt initiated a massive distribution program for food and other essentials. The neediest people qualified for assistance and were put on the Government role. Recipients of these provisions were "on relief". My family was on the list.

Once a month, on a Saturday, we kids hiked to town to pick up our allotment of commodities from a large panel truck parked in front of the school house. It was filled with dried prunes, powdered eggs, powdered milk, unbleached flour, dry beans, white rice and fifty pound sacks of potatoes. There were also some unglamorous dresses and denim pants and occasionally gray woolen blankets. It took

/

Illustration 27: The first Welfare Exchange food distribution in Hurricane was in 1938. (Photo: Wm. R. Palmer, 1940. Courtesy So. Utah Univ, Sherratt Library, Special Collections.)

several of us older kids to carry it all home. On all the brown paper packaging was stamped in bold black lettering: NOT TO BE SOLD. Although I was grateful to receive help of any kind, I was old enough to be ashamed and humiliated by "going public" with our poverty. Everyone in town was not as impoverished as we, nor did everyone have such a large family.

President Roosevelt also created the WPA (Work Projects Administration), the CCC (Civilian Conservation Corps) and other similar programs to provide employment for destitute people in the nation.

My dad got a job with the WPA and worked on the construction of the mile-long tunnel in Zion National Park, which was twenty-eight miles from Hurricane. A special bus provided transportation. His wages were thirty dollars a month and it was enough to get the electricity turned

Illustration 28: View from tunnel, east end; Zion National Park. (Photo: Wm. R. Palmer, 1940. Courtesy So. Utah Univ, Sherratt Library, Special Collections.)

back on in our house. Enough to get hooked up to the town's clean water pipeline. We were finally able to use our long-yearned-for bathroom, although there still wasn't any hot water in there.

Things didn't magically change for us overnight. Thirty dollars a month paid for the power and water but not much more. I was mortified when I couldn't start school on time in the fall. I would be in the seventh grade and had no shoes. A few boys did go to school barefoot. But not girls. It was nothing to go to town barefoot in the summer, and have to dash from shade to shade to keep from blistering the soles of our feet, but it was just too crude for girls to go to school like that.

Our grim struggle continued into the mid-thirties when the loan company gave up on us and confiscated our house. Grandpa Hall could have helped my dad save our house from the loan company. But he didn't.

Grandpa had a reputation for stinginess. He was considered tight-hided. He passed on this stingy trait to his sons—every one of them inherited it.

My dad never had any cash on hand, even when he had a little in the bank, and asking him for money was a source of shame for me.

Rumor has it that one of my uncles was so stingy, he'd climb over the gate so he wouldn't wear out the hinges. Rumor also has it another uncle could only afford one light bulb, so he unscrewed it and moved it to the socket in the next room he wanted to light up.

They weren't the only ones who could pinch a penny. When I was about twelve years old, I worked for our neighbor, who's husband owned a department store. I cleaned her house all day Saturday, for the rate of ten cents an hour. After ten hours labor, I had earned a dollar.

When it came time to pay, she was short a dime, and to my anguish, she said, “oh well, it's only worth ninety cents.” I went home crushed. She could have easily said, “I owe you a dime”. It seems I never forgave her for that.

From the eyes of a teenager, it was all about me. On a root level I understood poverty and all its symptoms and ramifications. I understood the chore of providing for a large family. But on the surface, I simply felt humiliated most of the time.

Home is a Four Room Shack

My father was able to trade a piece of land for a little old, shack-y, four-room frame house at the north end of town, a mile from downtown. We could not avoid getting plenty of exercise. The walking and running to school was undoubtedly good for us.

We began anew with no water piped into the house and no bathroom. We carried buckets full of water from an outside tap. In winter, the tap was wrapped in gunny-sacks to keep it from freezing. The water buckets were put on a wooden bench inside the kitchen by the back door. Bathing continued in the old tin tub on Saturday nights.

At last. Good fortune came our way in the form of being on the list for a government out-house. We qualified! We were ecstatic! This government issue was a beautiful little ship-lap wood structure painted a lovely gray. There was even a cement floor under it (allowing for the hole in the ground) and it had a decent door with a latch that worked. It was certainly a charming little building—by far the nicest structure on the lot. It was installed by the WPA guys.

The house, on the other hand, had a different kind of charm. It was quite possibly one of a kind. It did have electricity, thank goodness. We could at least see its discrepancies and short-comings by the light of a low-watt light globe. And we need not trip on the step up into the girl's bedroom.

The outside kitchen door, which acted as the front door, was fastened shut by a leather strap about six inches long which was nailed to the inside edge about where a doorknob would normally be. The other end had a slit about an inch long which hooked on a nail on the door jamb which protruded a half inch or so. It kept the door snugly in place. The door was actually made of boards with two cross-pieces to hold them together. Leather 'hinges" fastened the door on the jamb.

On the outside was another strap set-up so you could leave the door shut when you left home. When the door got too loose, a leather strip was nailed to the inside of the jamb to make it snug again. Our concern was to get the door to stay shut without locking family members out. Getting it to stay shut was sometimes tricky. There was no such thing as locking a door in those days. It was many years later before anyone in Hurricane thought of locking their doors. As it was with the strap, anyone else could have gotten in the same way we did. They never did. There was nothing in there that they could not have done better by somewhere else. Even if they did enter, they would not have found anything worth pilfering. Or perhaps if they did enter, they must have seen our plight and felt pity. There was really nothing to steal at our house.

Our closets—I use the term loosely—consisted of a board nailed flat on the wall. Every few inches a nail was pounded in part way so that clothes could be hung on them. We each had two nails to claim. That was plenty.

Another unique feature of this little house was a small cellar which was located under the kitchen. It was cool down there and was used for storing bottled fruit, flour, potatoes, apples and other food. The flour, fruits, and vegetables were put in gunny sacks and hung with baling wire hooked on nails to the cellar rafters to keep them safe from mice. Access was gained to this room by a trap door which was actually the floor of an open-ended pantry at the west end of the kitchen. This pantry had open shelves along one side and the far end, leaving room to open the trap door which, when open, hooked to a nail on the wall (with a leather strap, of course). We kept pans of milk on the shelves, allowing for the cream to rise. The closest light was a small watt bulb hanging from the ceiling in the opposite end of the kitchen. Only a dim reflection of it reached the interior of the pantry. After the eyes had adjusted to the darkness, it was usually possible to find what you were looking for.

I was a teenager when, one night, I dashed into the pantry to get something from the far end. The next thing I knew, I had plummeted eight feet down landing in the dirt in a terrible black void. Someone had left the trap door open. My panic was so stark that I sprang up out of there so fast that I literally was not on the ground long enough to get hurt. The momentum of my hurrying had carried me beyond the steep wooden steps so that I was not injured when I dropped into the dirt below.

I was not in the habit, or more truthfully, was not able to express myself, so did not scream during this sheer panic. I found my voice years later while in a little boat sailing through the Pirate's Cave at Magic Mountain with my young grandson. When the boat dropped over the edge to splash down way below, I let go of a long pent-up scream. It was not a pretty sound but I was grateful for it.

Changes

Even with the government programs, arduous times continued for us through the 'thirties'. Although things were a little improved since their inception, our family size had increased to nine children and we still barely scraped by. But now the older boys were able to help out more.

The bombing of Pearl Harbor on December 7, 1941, changed everything. All eligible boys and men between the ages of eighteen and forty-five were drafted and shipped off to war.

The aftermath of the bombing took us into the job market of prosperity and the productivity of World War II, when there was suddenly more to be done than there were people to do it. Many women as well, joined the military through womens' auxiliaries. Those left behind worked full-time making ammunition and war machines. Although there was plenty of rationing, it was now for a common cause, not a common plight of dire need.

The Depression was over.

In its place,

WAR.

Epilogue

Adding insult to injury, the second year into the war our little frame house caught fire and burned to the ground. All we saved was what we were wearing. The kitchen stove dropped through into the cellar, and later, there in the oven, we discovered some badly burned bread.

Everything went into the war effort. Through the Church, however, my dad was able to get a few loads of lumber to build us a new house. In the meantime, we had found a small vacant house we could live in while building the new one.

Today

Growing up with an eye to what was essential causes me to flinch when I see my grown children and other people turn the hot water tap on at the kitchen sink then walk around the room doing something else before they get back to it—not only wasting water, but HOT water. I also notice a lot of wanton disregard and wasting of food. We recently had a family reunion and I was shocked at how much food the kids left on their plates. It could be that the poverty mentality is still exaggerated in me but it does seem a shame to waste our valuable resources.

Now I find that those days of surviving my growing up years still prevail in my approach to life. I persist in doing difficult things, even when it isn't reasonable or necessary.

Most days, I work outside pulling or hoeing weeds on my two acres of land in Northern Arizona. Determined to beautify this place, and fill in some muddy spots, I even move rocks around. In my trundle cart, wheelbarrow, or using buckets, I haul cinders to make a rock garden and to cover the clay soil for my parking lot. I even maintain the off-road path in front of my fence for the mail lady. They are *lava* cinders, of course, reminiscent of my past.

I believe that working and being continually active is what keeps me strong, healthy and alert.

At eighty-five I completed an eight-month course in once-a-week line dancing—round trip to Hurricane, sixty miles. I drive very well, thank you, and with no glasses. At eighty-six, I just signed up for line dancing again, and have remembered the steps. It appears that I am finally coming out of my shell. I am friendly and finally not shy.

I have learned how to be healthy through being diligent in studying nutritional facts and living them the best I can. I sometimes do yoga and occasionally do some hiking. Not many others have to wait for me on the trail.

In my spare time, I do some painting, mostly landscapes. I don't play my violin anymore. I still consider myself a beginner at playing piano, although since I know chords, I can play to my satisfaction by ear. In addition, I read and always have a puzzle book on hand.

I have made a snuggly quilt for every member of my family, and most of their spouses. With six children, nine grandchildren and ten great-grandchildren now expanding the family, that is a bunch of quilts!

In the house, if furniture needs moving, I move it. If a shelf needs building, I build it. I'm thrifty and I don't take modern conveniences for granted.

Since I never had it easy as a child, I don't expect things to be necessarily easy now, and I just go on doing what needs to be done. Although I no longer experience icy wind blowing through cracks in the walls of my house, I know how to build a fire in my little wood-burning stove where it's cozy, warm, and helps to erase the chill of the past.

What were the Good Old Days, really, compared to today? We are all so spoiled. Perhaps the lyrics from the song, *Anticipation*, by Carly Simon, say it best:

"*These* Are *the Good Old Days*."

Appendix A: Photos

Here are some supplemental photos, since I decided to include photos which aren't necessarily relevant to my story: my large Hall family may enjoy the pictures of Halls; other people may find someone recognizable in the school photos from Rockville and other groups from that area, or you may find them historically interesting.

My daughter discovered other 'people' pictures at the Sherratt Library, Special Collections Dept., and decided we should add them before they are lost to history, since most of the people in William L. Crawford's images are not identified. Please go on-line and browse the Digital Collection, and if you find photos of your ancestors, the staff there can create a high-resolution copy for you at reasonable cost.

Illustration 29: Two Men at Peach Display, August 19, 1914. (Photo: Courtesy Victor Hall)

Illustration 23 : Bradshaw House built 1906-1908. As the first permanent house in Hurricane, it was used for Sunday School, as a hotel, boarding house, and meeting house. Listed on the National Historic Register, it is located at 85 S. Main Street. (Photo: Wm. L. Crawford. Courtesy So. Utah University, Sherratt Library, Special Collections)

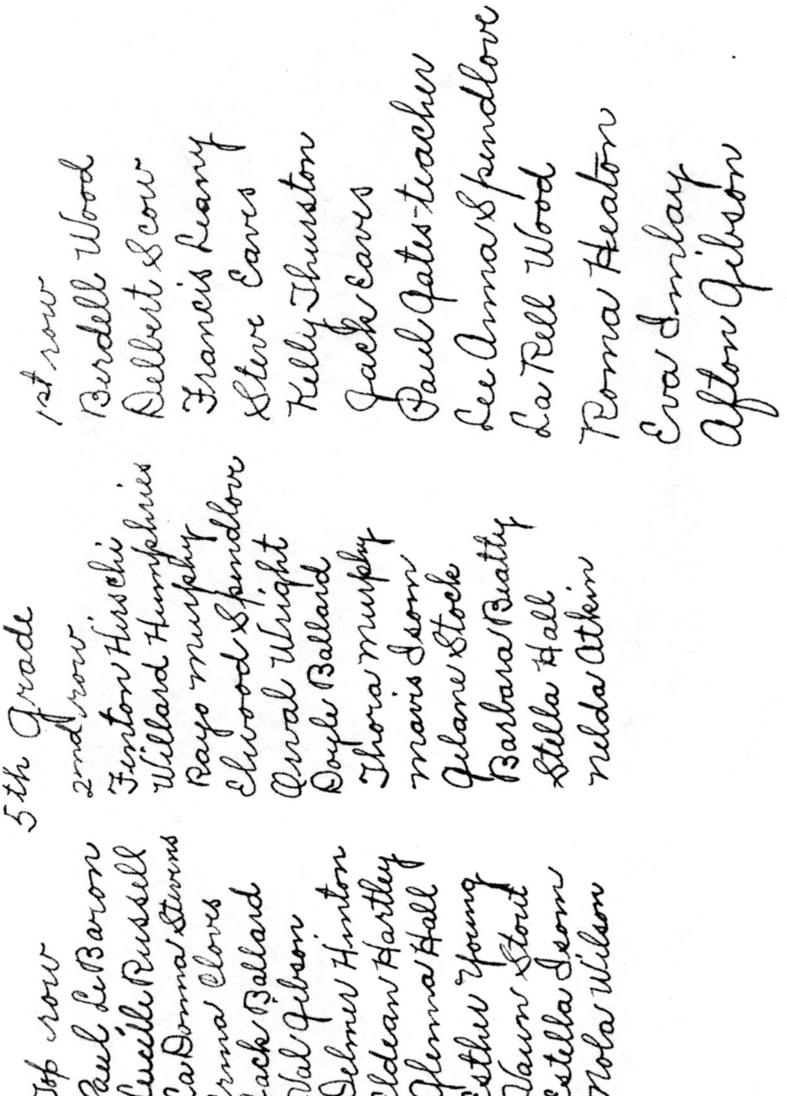
Top row
Paul LeBaron
Lucille Russell
LaDonna Stevens
Erma Cloves
Jack Ballard
Val Gibson
Delmer Hinton
Eldean Hartley
Glenna Hall
Esther Young
Vaun Stout
Estella Isom
Nola Wilson

5th Grade
2nd row
Fenton Hirschi
Willard Humphries
Rayo Murphy
Elwood Spendlove
Orval Wright
Doyle Ballard
Thora Murphy
Mavis Isom
Jelane Stocks
Barbara Beatty
Stella Hall
Nelda Atkin

1st row
Berdell Wood
Delbert Scow
Francis Leany
Steve Eaves
Kelly Thurston
Jack Eaves
Paul Gates-teacher
Lee Anna Spendlove
La Rell Wood
Roma Heaton
Eva Imlay
Afton Gibson

Illustration 31: Mr. Gates class. My mothers handwriting. It was a small town so we all knew everyone and their brothers and sisters, parents, aunts and uncles. My mother even knew most peoples birth dates.
—From page 57

Illustration 33: Horatio Pickett Extended Family. 1911 Left to Right

Back Row: Charles Workman, Ann (my mother), Eldon Workman, Philene, Paul.

Center Row: dau. Josephine (Pickett) Workman holding her dau. Eloise, dau. Susanna (Pickett) Gubler, step-brother "Uncle Sanjo," wife Philena holding dau. Una, Horatio Pickett.

Front Row: Carl Workman, Ruth Gubler, W. Tell (asleep), Hazel Workman, dau. LaVern, Rosalba Gubler.

Horatio Pickett was an only child of Susanna Mehitable Rogers who married 1) Sangiovanni, 2) Pickett, 3) Keate. Susanna left Wm. Pickett when Horatio was a baby and the marriage was annulled. She then came to Salt Lake.

Horatio's first wife died leaving a grown family, and Philena stepped in as his 2nd wife. Ann was a child of the 2nd family.

Josephine (family members may remember her as Aunt Dodie) belonged to the first family and married Charles Workman.

For the fascinating story of Susanna Mehitable Rogers, Read: "In Search of Living Water, by Jane Rae Fuller Topham . http://jkrogers.com/Art%20Work/In%20Search%20Of%20Living%20Water.pdf

Illustration 34: Family of Alfred Hall, Rockville, Utah, about 1904. Left to right, back row: Lafe, Hilda, Harvey, Alvin; Middle row: Roy, Alfred (father), Julia Hansen Hall (mother), Merrill; Front row: Clint, Nora, Vern (Photo: Wm. L. Crawford, Courtesy Sherratt Library Special Collections)

Alfred was born in Salt Lake City in 1858, and came to Rockville in the early 1860's with his parents, John Charles Hall and Keziah deGrey.

The 1880 Census shows a Julia Hanson [sp] on the same page as the Halls. Alfred, age 21. She is listed with the Joseph A. Smith household, as their servant, age 20. Her mother died in Rockville,1894 and her father died in New Mexico, 1906..

Illustration 35: Rockville School, c. 1893-94

Rockville School

People identified top to bottom and left to right.

Top Row: David Stout, Dan Dennett; 6th row: Charles Petty, Irving Stout, Dave Jennings, Frank Petty, Zira Terry, George Cole (Teacher), Henry Lay (or Lee), LaMar Stout, John (Cho) Dennett, Alfred (Ap) Bliss, LeRoy Hall;

5th Row: Mary Huber, Georganna Stout, Mary (Molly) Terry, Alice Brown, Ellen Lemmon, Annie Stout, Mishie Cox, Dora Hall, Arthur Hall;

4th Row: Hosea (Hate) Stout, Alice Stout, Cora Farnes, Fanny Farnes, Caroline Larsen, Zelpha Huber, Laura Stout, Jennie Petty, Daisy Stout, Rhoda Huber, Alfred (Top) Stout, Joe Farnes;

3rd Row: Dave Dennett, Lionel Stout, Ov Larsen, Cornelia (Neal) Larsen, Zelpha (Biff) Petty, Letitia Huber, Annie Jennings, Louie Beebe, Maude Langston, Will Stout, Harmer (Ham) Petty, Sam Larsen;

2nd Row: Johnnie Dalton, Zira Draper, Gretchen Stout, Mable Stout, Stella Stout, Trudie Dennett, Mandy Stout, Walter Stout, Alma Langston, Ella Langston, George Huber, Nate Petty, Jimmie Jennings;

1st Row: Emerald Stout, Merrill Hall, Retta Farnes, Stella Beebe, Lafe Hall, Eddie Dalton, Jessie Jennings, Pearl Dalton, Elmer Stout, Lester Dalton

(Photo: Wm. L. Crawford, Courtesy So. Utah University, Sherratt Library, Special Collections Dept.)

Illustration 36: Rockville School Not Identified (Photo: Wm. L Crawford. Courtesy, SUU Sherratt Library, Special Collections)

Illustration 37: Rockville School, none identified. (Photo: Wm. L. Crawford, Courtesy SUU Sherratt Library Special Collections)

Illustration 38: Unidentified Rockville Group(Photo: Wm. L. Crawford, Courtesy So. Utah. University, Sherratt Library, Special Collections)

Illustration 39: Rockville School. Dave Hirschi, Teacher, c. 1897 (Photo: Courtesy Victor Hall)

Illustration 40: Rockville Beauties, c. 1915 (Photo: Wm. L. Crawford, Courtesy SUU Sherratt Library, Special Collections)

Rockville Beauties.

Back row: Mary DeMille, Rachel Hirschi, Fern Jones, Alice (Brown) Russell, Edna Langston, Marsha Terry, Naomi DeMille, Edna Russell, Madge Jones, Emaline Millet;

Middle row: Carrie Lemmon, Susie Hirschi, Mae Dalton, Maine Stout Hirschi, Vera Dennett Allred, Louie Ballard?;

Front row: Myrtle Dalton Hirschi, Irene Russell, Augusta Jennings, Nona May DeMille, Grace DeMille Hirschi.

Note from scan technician: "The picture is not reversed. The flag is suspended incorrectly." (Photo: Wm. L Crawford, Courtesy So. Utah University, Sherratt Library, Special Collections)

Illustration 41: First Welfare Distribution in Hurricane, 1938. (Photo: Wm.L. Palmer, Courtesy Sherratt Library Special Collections)

Illustration 42: Rockville Buggy. East of Apple Valley, this rugged road from Big Plains to Rockville is still used. The view is looking north toward the Smithsonian Butte. (Photo: Wm. L. Crawford. Courtesy So. Utah University, Sherratt Library, Special Collections.)

Illustration 43: Close up.

Illustration 44: Five Cousins. Alvin Hall back left, with Dalton's c. 1890-91 (Photo: J..J. Booth & Black, Thelma Hall Collection)

Illustration 45: Children of Alfred and Julia Hall.

Harvey Hall, seated, Alvin Hall, Hilda Hall, about 1897. (Photo Courtesy Victor Hall, son of Harvey.)

Appendix B: Interesting 1924 Events

The year 1924 was notable for many innovative and important occurrences:

- First Winter Olympic Games held in France.
- Johnny Weismuller won two gold medals in swimming then went to Hollywood to star in Tarzan.
- Calvin Coolidge was elected president.
- Ford Motor Company produced its millionth car.
- Willem Einthoven, a Dutch scientist, won the Nobel Prize for inventing the Electrocardiogram.
- Zenith produced its first portable radio for consumers. It weighed 14.6 pounds, cost $230, and fit in a suitcase.
- Indy 500 race car topped out at an incredible speed of 98.23 mph.
- The 28th Boston Marathon was won by Clarence DeMar.
- Kentucky Derby was won by Black Gold, who was finally inducted into the Horses Hall of Fame in 1989.
- Some popular songs were: *I'll See You In My Dreams, Sweet Georgia Brown,* and *Hard Hearted Hannah.*
- Notable Birthdays: Lauren Bacall, Marlon Brando, Lee Iacocca, Jimmy Carter, Henry Mancini, and Gloria Vanderbilt.

Most of this information was pulled from a booklet called the *Year You Were Born 1924*. For some reason it failed to mention my birth. Glenna Hall, born August 19th, 1924 at 7a.m. In St. George, Utah.

Appendix C: References and Further Reading

1) A good reference article online.
   http://www.southernutahhistory.com/history

HISTORY OF THE HURRICANE BENCH (Hurricane, Utah)

A Synopsis By: Bruce W. Church

His article draws from other works:

* De Mille, Janice Force, *Portraits of the Hurricane Pioneers*, Homestead Publishers 1976.

* Larson, Andrew Karl, I was Called To Dixie, The Deseret News Press, 1961.

* Washington County Chapter of the Daughters of Utah Pioneers, Under the Dixie Sun, Garfield County News press, Panquitch, Utah, 1950.

Authors Note: The referenced sources have been used extensive[ly] & liberally with some text taken directly from their work. Credit for the information mainly belongs to the various referenced authors. This current effort is an attempt to summarize the information available and shorten it for a quick easy read of the history of the Hurricane Bench.

Mr. Church, an expert in molecular radiobiology, grew up in LaVerkin, and has now returned to the area. Visit his web site for information on the History of the Nevada Test Site and links to radioactive effects on health on "downwinders." http://www.southernutahhistory.com/about w

2) DVD created by the Sons of Utah Pioneers details the *Story of the Hurricane Canal*, written by Victor Hall. Historical sources listed:

   a. Slack, Martin, Letter
   b. Evans, Rick L., *When Water Came to Hurricane,* Improvement Era Magazine, 1937
   c. Stratton, Alice Gubler, *The Story of the Hurricane Canal,* Manuscript.
   d. Stout, Dell, Hurricane, *Then and Now*, 1999.
   e. Reeve, Paul W., *Little Oasis in the Desert*, Whirlwind Press, Salt Lake City, UT 1996

3) Online Article by Wesley P. Larsen

   http://www.onlineutah.com/hurricanehistory.shtml

He lists source references:

See: Daughters of Utah Pioneers, Washington County Chapter, "Under Dixie Sun" (1950); Andrew Karl Larson, I Was Called to Dixie (1961); Angus M. Woodbury, "A History of Southern Utah and its National Parks," Utah Historical Quarterly 12 (1944).

4) Online reference from Univ. of Maryland transcripts:

Father Escalante's Journal October 15th entry:

http://www.mith2.umd.edu/eada/gateway/diario/diary.html

5) Online reference from DesertUSA web site:

http://www.desertusa.com/mag99/sep/papr/escalante.html

6) Online reference from Washington County [Utah] Historical Society: http://wchsutah.org/documents/documents.htm

Juanita Brooks Lecture Series 27,

Southern Paiute Relations With Their Early Dixie Mormon Neighbors, by Edward Leo Lyman, a publication of Dixie State College, St. George, Utah, 2010

http://wchsutah.org/documents/juanita-brooks-lecture-27.pdf

7) Biography of Horatio Pickett, Hall family papers.

8) Almonds *"The most flavorsome almonds are bitter almonds (as opposed to "sweet" almonds). They have the strongest scent and are the most popular in many countries. But there is one problem: they are full of cyanide. Before consumption, bitter almonds must be processed to remove the poison. Despite this requirement, some countries make the sale of bitter almonds illegal . . . As an alternative, you can use the pip from an apricot stone which has a similar flavor and poison content. Heating destroys the poison. In fact, you may not know that it is now illegal in the USA to sell raw almonds – all almonds sold are now heat-treated to remove traces of poison and bacteria."*

http://listverse.com/2009/01/06/top-10-poisonous-foods-we-love-to-eat/

9) Bradshaw House/ Hotel, 85 S. Main Street, Hurricane, UT. http://wchsutah.org/homes/bradshaw-home-hotel.htm

Alaina Newhart is a third generation Utah pioneer. As a quiet, shy, person she did not participate much, but observed the lives that went on around her as a town was being formed with little chance of survival.

At 86, she felt compelled to publish her story. Still overcoming the challenges of her rugged childhood she is definitely a survivor. Alaina makes her home in Northern Arizona.

The Man Behind The Camera

Thank you,

William Louis Crawford

For documenting our lives.